DERRIDA ON THE THRESH

By the same author

BEYOND METAPHYSICS?
The Hermeneutic Circle in Contemporary Continental
Philosophy

DERRIDA
ON THE THRESHOLD OF
SENSE

John Llewelyn

MACMILLAN

First published 1986
Reprinted 1989

Published by
THE MACMILLAN PRESS LTD
Houndmills, Basingstoke, Hampshire RG21 2XS
and London
Companies and representatives
throughout the world

Printed by Antony Rowe Ltd, Chippenham, Wiltshire

British Library Cataloguing in Publication Data
Llewelyn, John
Derrida on the threshold of sense.
1. Derrida, Jacques
I. Title
194   B2430.D484
ISBN 0-333-38749-X (hardcover)
ISBN 0-333-38750-3 (paperback)

*This book is dedicated to my brothers David and Howard,
and to the grandmother, mother, father, uncles and aunts
who dedicated themselves to us.*

The centre is the threshold

Edmond Jabès
cited by
Jacques Derrida
L'Ecriture et la différence
(Editions Seuil)

It is always a significant question to ask about any philosopher: what is he afraid of?

Iris Murdoch
The Sovereignty of Good

Contents

Acknowledgements

Chapter 1 and Section II of Chapter 6 of this book are adapted with kind permission from, respectively, 'Thresholds', published in *Derrida and Differance* (University of Warwick: Parousia Press, 1985), and 'Heidegger's Kant and the Middle Voice', published in *Time and Metaphysics* (University of Warwick: Parousia Press, 1982), both edited by David Wood and Robert Bernasconi. I thank them, Jacques Derrida, David Farrell Krell, David Robinson and John Sallis for help with matters bibliographical, philosophical or linguistic, J. Hillis Miller for the very practical manner in which he continued to show interest in my project, the British Academy (Small Grants Research Fund in the Humanities), the University of Edinburgh and the Director and staff of the Institut Francophone de Paris for enabling me to go to France to come to me. I am grateful to Margo Taylor for preparing the index and to Tim Farmiloe and Margaret Leach for their expert guidance across the threshold between typescript and print. Above all I am in debt to my dear wife Maggie for her consistent help with 'all those little matters on which the daily happiness of private life depends'.

J.L.

Preface

> It will therefore be necessary to make a detailed reconnaissance of the frontier.
>
> Jacques Derrida, *Dissemination*

The writings of Jacques Derrida are parasitic. Chapter 5 of this exposition of some of those writings is about what is said in saying this. Suffice it to say at this preliminary stage that his writings are an unraveling of the writings of others, a kind of *lecture expliquée*. I aim to explicate in turn his readings of some of the texts of Hegel, Husserl, Heidegger, Saussure, Lévi-Strauss, Austin and Searle. On those readings these texts are shown not to make complete sense. They dis-seminate themselves. They are, as grammarians say of certain sorts of ill-formed sentences, broken-backed; they do not construe. Both because of themselves and in spite of themselves they de-construct themselves. I attempt to explain why Derrida holds that this deconstruction is structurally necessary, why it is not merely a matter of chance, a haphazard throw of the dice.

It is a matter of 'matter'. Not of matter as opposed to form, but as what makes hylo-morphism possible. At least as a preliminary, it is helpful to place Derrida's writings in the context of those in which Anaximander, Anaximenes and Heraclitus, for instance, treat of prime matter, and of Plato's treatment of *apeiron*, the aorist, the imperfect and unlimited in the *Philebus*, the *Republic*, the *Sophist*, and the parts of the *Timæus* which speak of the cosmological receptacle, *chôra*. The 'Platonic' background is crucial because the topic of the unlimited and indefinite overlaps with the quest for definitions or analyses. According to Derrida, no definition and no last essential analysis is to be found. So can Derrida's programme be assimilated to the investigations of the later Wittgenstein where it is brought out that the similarity of instances of the same concept is usually, perhaps ultimately always, only one of family resemblance? We shall note the risk incurred in saying that there is a family resemblance between the projects of Derrida and Wittgenstein, but we shall not deny that there is a remoter resemblance. There is also a resemblance between Derrida on sense, Peirce on signs and Quine on the indeterminacy of radical translation. This will assist those of us who come to Derrida with the philosophical ethos predominant in English-speaking countries to feel less like innocents abroad.

Yet I doubt that Derrida can be domesticated. We have not seen it all before. One of the things some of us have not seen before is how 'Continental' our recent anglophone philosophy is, and not only on account of the Jewish exodus from the Continent or because Frege was German and Wittgenstein Viennese. The philosophical common market is an exchange. That most properly academic of Oxonians, John Austin, turns out on Derrida's portrayal of him to be the spitting image of Nietzsche, the 'frivolous', 'infantile', 'petulant' Continental litterateur some of us are only now beginning to take seriously. Nor do some of us take very seriously Austin's own declaration that he is doing linguistic phenomenology. We shall see how Derrida endorses this declaration and how he supports his claim that some of the presuppositions of John Searle's theory of speech acts are shared with the earnest phenomenological theories of meaning advanced by Hegel, Husserl, Heidegger and Saussure and with their and his frivolous Parisian deconstructor Jacques Derrida. We shall see this when we have read some of the German and French texts at Derrida's prompting. By then we may be prepared to be uncertain about what is serious and what is frivolous, what philosophy and what literature. Indeed, by then we shall have become acquainted with Derrida's exposure of an uncertainty principle under the foundation stone of everything he deconstructs. The uncertainty is an undecidability over what is inside and what is out, over thresholds. It is discovered too under the threshold which is called the preface of a book. This was detected by Hegel and described in more than one of the prefaces to his own books. Since the chapter that raises the curtain of this book is an introduction to Hegel's semiology and to Derrida's double reading of it, this preface would seem to be the proper place for some prefatory remarks on Hegel and Derrida on prefaces.

The minutiæ of Derrida's statement of the paradox of the Hegelian preface are detailed in 'Hors Livre – Préfaces' of

Dissemination. Put baldly, as one is permitted to put things in
prefaces, the paradox is the following. Hegelian philosophy is the
systematic self-development of the concretely universal concept.
In that case, a preface to philosophy is peripheral and pre-lim-
inary, a mere *hors d'œuvre* outside the meal whose central course
is the guts of the book. It can give only such empirically historical particulars the preface you are now reading gives: pre-
prandial gossip about how this philosophical position is placed
in relation to that and about how unnecessary and noxious
prefaces are to philosophy as such because they create the false
impression that conclusions and positions can be understood
outside the dialectical process leading to them. However, in
Hegel's philosophy the systematic self-development is a movement to the universal via a process of rational *Aufhebung* which
both cancels and conserves the empirically historical particulars.
So the content of the preface of philosophy, although external, is
also necessarily internal. Further, have not the Prefaces and
Introductions of the *Phenomenology of Spirit* and of the *Science of
Logic* been taken up into the living context of the main text? For
they were written, after all, after all. In time they are postscripts,
composed after the climax of absolute knowing. Or, since the
conceptually historical crescendo which leads up to that climax
and follows the official preface in space, nevertheless precedes it
in time, is not this, the spatially central part of the volume, really
a prelude prefatory to the part entitled Preface?

This paradox is inevitable, Derrida tries to show, once we
start by opposing, for example, the rational and the empirical,
form and content, the intelligible and the sensible, mind and
matter, the signifier and the signified, the central and the peripheral, the *ergon* and the *parergon*, the serious and the parasitic,
philosophy and literature, mention and use (in the title of a
preface, this one or those where Hegel and Derrida treat of the
topic of the preface, is the word mentioned or is it used?). Not
that Hegel and the other 'Platonist' thinkers whose texts we are
to re-read in the course of this study, least of all Plato himself,
are without excuse in underestimating the complexity of these
dualisms. They and we are subject to transcendental illusion.
However, now and then, consciously or unconsciously (another
dualism which invites deconstruction), the illusoriness is recognised. Derrida's acknowledgement that this recognition is implicit in the texts he deconstructs is a mark of the fact that to

deconstruct is not to destroy except in the sense in which to destroy is for Heidegger to disillusion by dissolution. As Derrida does not fail to mention, Hegel comments in the Preface to the *Phenomenology of Spirit* on the externality and formalism of the thesis-antithesis-synthesis formula as this is employed by Kant and Schelling. Hegel sets out to interiorise and vivify this merely external triadic *Konstruktion*. In doing so he is not criticising the Critical philosophy in a purely negative fashion or simply rejecting Schelling's philosophy of nature. To do that would be to surrender his own conception of philosophy. Nor does Derrida reject the Hegelian conception. To oppose or contradict it simply would be to endorse its dialectic of *Aufhebung* which itself hinges on contradiction. So although Derrida believes it is too late or too early for us, whoever we are, to co-operate in the dialectic of *Er-innerung*, whether Hegelian or Platonic, it would be a mistake to suppose that he is either turning the dialectic upside down or advancing it a stage by subsuming the inside under the outside. It is this very threshold between the inside and the outside which Derridian deconstruction turns inside out – or, as it is more accurate to say, is shown to turn itself inside out: for, let us be clear from the start, when Derrida refers to the deconstruction or dissemination of something, the 'of' marks a genitive which is both objective and subjective.

Note on where to go from here: Those who feel more at home in the philosophical idiom of, say, Frege, than they do in that of, say, Heidegger, may prefer to read Chapters 5 to 7 and the Postscript before having a go at the other parts of this book.

1 Dialectical Semiology

> I was coming to that
>
> Robert Graves, *Welsh Incident*

I THRESHOLDS

Hegel's semiology is dialectical. The sense of the sign is a middle between the sensible and the intelligible, as the Kantian schema is a sensible concept in the imagination.[1] In the sign itself the internalised essence of external particulars is incorporated and re-externalised in objective thought in itself, that is to say in the public memory of a spoken language.

The imagination (*Einbildungskraft*) is a threshold where a rite of passage is performed which confers a right of way between sensibility and sense. Its raw materials are the images of externally intuited particulars. These images are appropriated and stored in the subliminal pit or reservoir of private memory (*Erinnerung*). Images, which can be reproduced more or less at will, are a relatively concrete kind of representation. Their content or material, like that of any other intellectual representation, is given and found, as a matter of fact, to be. 'The representation is the middle term in the syllogism of the elevation (*Erhebung*) of intelligence, the link between the two significations of self-relatedness, namely that of being and that of universality, which are distinguished in consciousness as object and subject'.[2] Images are 'more universal' than intuitions.[3] But they become general ideas only when they are associated by the spontaneous activity of the subject. This is not an association which produces a merely mechanical collocation of an external image and an internal general idea. The unity produced is not neuter, *ne-uter*, neither just the one nor just the other. The general idea is the subjection of the relatively external ob-jecthood of the image

1

which otherwise simply happens to be there. The general idea 'makes itself into the image's soul'. It inwardises itself and in the image becomes for itself, since it becomes manifest in the image that has now taken on the form of a work of art in which, for example, the eagle stands for Jupiter's strength.

This pictorial product of the creative imagination (*Phantasie*) is pro-phetic, no more than an annunciation of language, an apocalypse. The internal essence of intuited external particulars assumes a new form of externality when it becomes objective thought in itself (*Denken*) as a sign in the public memory (*Gedächtnis, Mnemosyne*) of language. Signs, in comparison with symbols, are arbitrary and more original in that whereas the eagle is made to symbolise the strength of Jupiter because of what is thought to be a natural resemblance, no such resemblance is thought to hold between a cockade or a flag or a tombstone and what they severally signify. Hegel's sign corresponds to the body in one of Saussure's (rejected) analogies for the signifier, where the signified meaning is the soul. The sign is 'the pyramid into which a foreign soul has been conveyed, and where it is conserved'.[4] The pyramid is the semaphore of the sign, Derrida observes, alluding to the connections made in the *Cratylus* between *sêma*, sign or tomb, and *sôma*, prison house or body. It is also worthy of note that in Homer *sôma* means corpse, *Körper*, and only later, as in Plato, comes to be used both of that and of the living body, the *Leib*. Hegel must have thought that this development in the history of Greek oiled the wheels of the semiological dialectic, the Janus logic of which Derrida parses as follows:

> The tomb is the life of the body as sign of death, the body as the other of the soul, of the animated psyche, of the living breath. But the tomb is also that which shelters life and keeps it reserved in its thesaurus marking its continuation elsewhere. Family vault: *oikèsis*. It consecrates the disappearance of life in testifying to its persistence. So it also shelters it from death. It averts (*avertit*) and adverts to (*avertit*) the possible death of the soul. [*M* 95 (82)]

The sign, regarded as the composite of signifier and signified, the animated signifier, is a monument both of life in death and death in life. It is the threshold between life and life after or, better, through death, facing in both directions, *à double sens*. Signification, sign-making, has the dia-lecticality of any other *Aufhebung* of the phenomenology of spirit. The transition from the physical body to the spiritual body and from the private meaning stored in the dark underground reservoir of the unconscious to the public meaning manifest in the medium of discourse is a passing away which is also a passing on, a revocation which is also a reinvocation, a destruction and a reconstruction. We can look forward to witnessing the destruction of the fabric of this semiologic when Derrida teases out its threads and reconstrues them with yarns suspended on the tenterhooks of what he calls deconstruction.

The passage across a dialectical threshold is negation and affirmation. The sign is the deposition of the symbol and the proposition of its truth. It is the symbol internalised (*erinnert*) and surpassed. Whereas the pyramid is the sign of signification, the Sphinx is the symbol of symbolism. The animal form of the Sphinx mirrors the natural forms of hieroglyphics on account of which they were polysemic and enigmatic even for the Egyptians. And the pyramid is the sign of only a degenerate form of signification, since as an object in space it is naturally taken to stand for the written sign. The written sign is less fully linguistic than the phonetic sign in, for instance, the alphabetic language with which the Greeks 'deconstituted' [*M* 116 (99)] the hieroglyphic symbolism of the Egyptians. Hegel dramatises this epoch-making translation in terms of Œdipus's de-ciphering the enigma of the Sphinx and 'destroying' the Sphinx in so doing. This promotion of the spoken word at the expense of writing is, as Derrida reminds us in 'La pharmacie de Platon', a dominant theme in the *Phædrus* and other dialogues of Plato. It may strike one as odd that in spite of the phonologism which Plato and Hegel share, the former appears to hold mathematics in much greater esteem than does the latter. Think of the Pythagoreanism of the *Timæus*. For Hegel Pythagoreanism is a term of abuse for the Chinese philosophy which gives priority to the abstract sensuousness of spatiality in taking as its paradigm the mathematical *calculus* whose very name indicates kinship with *glyptography*. The air of paradox is reduced if we recall that in the *Republic* and elsewhere the mathematicals are intermediate between sensible things and the intelligible Ideas; as for Kant the schema of number is a medium between sensible particulars and concepts; as for Hegel number is the other of the concept and therefore facilitates its emergence because it is the pure thought of thought's own extraneation: 'sie ist der *reine Gedanke* der eigenen Entäusserung des Gedankens'.[5] The paradoxicality evaporates completely if we think of Plato's Pythagoreanism as a theory of musical harmony, since for Hegel music 'makes the point of transition between the abstract spatial sensuousness of painting and the abstract spirituality of poetry.'[6]

Furthermore, sound is the 'incipient ideality of matter which appears no longer as spatial but as temporal ideality.'[7] It is, in Derrida's words, the becoming time of space [*M* 8 (8)]. Time is space *aufgehoben*, passed over, displaced, surpassed, *gewesen*: the essence (*Wesen*) of space, its truth; in Derrida's words again, what space will have meant ('*aura voulu dire*'). What goes on (*se passe*) between the affect and the '*sein-g*' [*Glas* 51 (58)], the entire process of consignment from pit to pyramid, from sensible intuition via subconscious private image and natural symbol to freely instituted sign, homes in on meaning which has put behind it the gap between itself and the symbol or sign by which it is re-presented. Symbol and sign 'must in their turn be thought (*aufgehoben*, *relevés*, recuperated) by the living concept, by languageless language, language which has become the thing itself, the inner voice whispering in the mind's ear the identity of the name (and) of being' [*M* 125 (106)]. This is the phenomenological voice of logocentrism. The centre of logocentrism is the idea or ideal of understanding (*entendement*) which hears itself speak (*s'entend parler*) in closest proximity to itself and in the immediate presence of its subject matter. The sign, the spirit incarnate, is the (p)re-presentation, the *Vor-stellung*, of absolute knowing as Christianity is the *Vor-stellung* of philosophy [*Glas* 40 (44)].

II   WHAT IS THE ABSOLUTE DIFFERENCE?

Jean Hyppolite, whose seminars Derrida took part in and whose works he frequently cites, asks of the language of philosophy '*Qui parle?*'

Who or what is speaking? The answer is neither 'one' [or 'das Man'] nor 'it' [or 'the id'], nor quite 'the I' or 'the we'. This name *dialectic* which Hegel has revived and interpreted and which designates a dialectic of things themselves, not an instrument of knowledge, is itself at the heart of this problem.

What is a philosophical presentation and what is its structure? It is remarkable that in trying to present the system of the articulations and determinations of thought Hegel saw both their objectivity – they are a universal consciousness of Being – and what opposes them to the thing itself, to Nature. The logos says also the absolute difference, but it is not itself absolute difference since this difference belongs as well [still (*encore*)] to the logos. Universal Knowledge therefore knows too its own limit. It measures the limits of signification or sense, the quota of *non-sense* that still invests signification, what Hegel saw as the rapport of Logos and Nature, the play of their identity and difference. For Hegel this was not a question of a negative theology, of a meaning so to speak beyond meaning, but of an irremediable finitude, a lost meaning (as one talks of a lost cause) which can never be completely recovered.[8]

Derrida knows the paper from which these sentences are extracted. He himself gave a paper at the Baltimore symposium at which it was tabled. He knows too what Hegel says about absolute difference. What does Derrida say about what Hegel says about this? Are what Derrida says and what Hyppolite says about what Hegel says in any way different?

In the section of the *Science of Logic* entitled '*Der absolute Unterschied*' Hegel tells us that absolute difference is 'the negativity which reflection has within it'. It is 'difference in and for itself, not difference resulting from anything external, but *self-related* (*sich auf sich beziehender*), therefore *simple* (*einfacher*) difference'. He writes of 'the *simple not*' and in the *Phenomenology of Spirit*, where it is more evident that his remarks have Kant and Fichte as their target, he refers to 'the simple *category*' and 'the simple *unity*', the essential unity of being and self-consciousness:

in other words, the category means this, that self-consciousness and being are the same essence, the same, not through comparison, but in and for themselves. It is only one-sided, spurious idealism that lets this unity come on the scene again as consciousness, on the one hand, confronted by an *in-itself*, on the other. But now this category or *simple* unity of self-consciousness and being possesses difference *in itself*; for its essence is just this, to be immediately one and selfsame in *otherness*, or in absolute difference.[9]

Hegel is distinguishing the opposition or otherness of absolute difference, which is a procedure of reflection and essence (*Wesen*), the been (*gewesen*), from the relative or comparative opposition of determinate beings. In the case of the latter the opposed beings are each opposed to the other and each has an immediately present being for itself. With absolute difference each other, since its otherness is reflected, is the other not only for itself but also in itself. As reflected difference it is posited as difference of itself from itself. This means that difference is both the whole in which it differentiates itself from its other, identity, and the moment, difference, which differentiates itself. In the section leading up to the one in which the *Science of Logic* spells out the logic of difference complementary formulæ are asserted of identity; for example: 'it is the whole, but, as reflective, it posits itself as its own moment, as positedness, from which it is the return into itself. It is only as such moment of itself that it is identity as such, as *determination* of simple equality with itself in contrast to absolute difference'.

The co-respondence between identity and difference is not a contradiction to be lamented. Although ordinary understanding abhors contradiction as nature abhors a vacuum, speculative thinking knows that contradiction is the principle that moves the world, *Was überhaupt die Welt bewegt*.[10] For when each of the opposed moments falls to the ground (*zugrunde geht*) speculative thinking realises the truth of what difference and identity have turned out to be, namely Ground, the more realised concept in which identity and difference are united. However,

We must be careful, when we say that the ground is the unity of identity and difference, not to understand by this unity an abstract identity. Otherwise we only change the name, while we still think the identity (of understanding) already seen to be false. To avoid this misconception we may say that the ground, besides being the unity, is also the difference of identity and difference. In that case in the ground, which promised at first to supersede the contradiction, a new contradiction seems to arise. It is, however, a contradiction which, so far from persisting quietly in itself, is rather the repulsion (*Abstossen*) of it from itself.[11]

If contradiction is the principle that moves the world, so is difference, in the two senses of *bewegt* Hegel plays on in the opening paragraphs of the Doctrine of Essence. There he announces that the truth of being is essence. Essence, *Wesen*, is timelessly past being, as suggested by the past participle, *gewesen*, of *sein* (which, it may be significant to semaphore in passing, is to Derrida suggestive of *sein-g*). This mediation of being by essence is the path (*Weg*) of knowing and the pathfinding motivation of being. This wordplay is compounded with one to the same effect on *Gang*, path, and *vergangenen*, past. And it is now timely to interpolate that while the Doctrine of Being treats of the timeless present of immediate being and the Doctrine of Essence treats of Being's mediated timeless past, these two doctrines comprising Objective Logic, the Subjective Logic of the Doctrine of the Concept treats of the sense in and into which Being was timelessly to come.

Derrida recognises this way-making activity of absolute difference. He endorses Koyré's reading of passages in the *Jena Logic* in which Hegel departs from his usual practice of using the word *Unterschied* for difference and speaks of an *absolut differente Beziehung* for which Koyré proposes the translation 'absolutely differentiating relation', where *differente* is given an active sense [*M* 14–15 (13–14)]. The activity in question in the pages Koyré cites is the activity of the simple present. The present is divided against itself, as is indicated by the German word for the present, *Gegenwart*. Its presence is *dichôs*, two-way, januarial (That's Shell that was). It has its deaths and entrances. Its simplicity is a onefoldness that is a once foldedness, a duplicity that gives itself away.

This simple, in this absolute negating, is the active, the infinite opposed to itself as an equal to itself; as negating it is as absolutely related to its opposite, and its activity, its simple negating, is a relation to its opposite, and the now is the immediately opposite of itself, its self-negating. While this limit sublates itself in its excluding or in its activity, what acts against and negates itself is rather the non-being of this limit. This immediate non-being in itself of the limit, this non-being opposed to itself as the active, or as that which rather is in itself and excludes its opposite, is the *future* which the now cannot resist; since it is the essence of the present which is in effect its own non-being . . . . The present is but the self-negating simple limit which, with its negative moments kept apart, is a relation between its excluding and that which does the excluding. This relation is presence [*Gegenwart* without a definite article] as [adopting Koyré's translation of *eine differente Beziehung*] a differentiating relation.[12]

Although Derrida endorses Koyré's transcription of *différente*, he denies that it does all of the jobs so far envisaged for *la différance*. Three of these are specified in the paper which has these words for a title. First, differance is the non-identity of differents. Secondly, it is the polemical productive activity of differends [*M* 8 (8)]. However, whereas the activity of Hegel's absolute difference is a kind of logical contradicting productive of meaning and truth, Derrida, although he often calls differance a contradiction, suggests we try to view differance as a conflict of forces or an allergy [*M* 8 (8), *Pos* 60 (101)]. This is already a violent displacement of Hegel even if we accept Hyppolite's interpretation cited above in which Hegel's absolute difference is, if we accept the English version of his words published in the transcript of the Baltimore symposium, 'the measure of meaninglessness that invests all meaning.' The risk run here is that of having the concept of meaninglessness get its meaning from its opposition to meaningfulness, thus binding it to the system of dialectical logic as firmly as a proposition which is false because self-contradictory is held within the analytic calculus of propositions. Hegel himself, Doctor Dialectic, would be the last to call this a risk. What is at risk is the plausibility of any attempt Hyppolite may be making to show that there is a something or a nothing which remains beyond the dialectic's pale, whether or not Hegel acknowledges this. The risk is reduced if we read his *non-sens* not as the contrary of the meaningful only, but as the metalinguistic excluder of both the meaningful and the meaningless. Derrida's re-reading of contradiction as a conflict of forces or of energies, instead of a conflict of concepts or propositions, is one way in which he tries to loosen the grip which the conception of dialectical difference and the metaphysics of meaning have on the project of differance. A conflict of forces or energies cannot meaningfully be said to be either meaningful or meaningless. This grip is further loosened by the third dimension of differance.

The third dimension of differance is postponement, deferment, delay, reservation or representation. Incidentally, if some of these words, the last two, for instance, appear to be at odds with the others, it will help to remember that they are two-faced vehicles of conflicting forces. Reservation is not just keeping but also keeping back and holding off. And 'representation' represents *Vor-stellung*. (Surely, in the appeal to such crosswordings Hegel is Derrida's past master?) But postponement, Derrida says, is not a power of the Greek *diapherein*. This loss in the most characteristically philosophical language is however compensated by *differre* in the less philosophical language of Latin. Despite Hegel's recourse in the *Jena Logic* to the Latinate *differente*, his thinking is, for Derrida, as it is for Heidegger, too Greek. It cannot, even with the help of Koyré's 'differentiation', summon up the force to perform the third operation of differance for which Derrida uses the non-terminal term 'temporisation'.

Nonetheless, Hyppolite's Hegel is reminiscent or evocative of the appendix differance supplies to Hegel's text. Was there a feedback from Derrida to Hyppolite, as when Wittgenstein was *in statu pupillari* to Russell? Or are we exaggerating the unfamiliarity in Hyppolite's reading? His references to the *non-sens* in Hegel are references to his opposition of knowing to being and of *logos* to nature. The second term of each of these pairs limits the former, and absolute knowing knows this limit. Now there is a singular sentence in the paper as published by Macksey and Donato: *Le logos dit aussi la différence absolue, mais il n'est pas lui-même la différence absolue car cette différence appartient encore au logos.* Did he not intend, it might be asked, and perhaps in his original manuscript say, that the difference belongs as well to *nature?* This would be in line with his answer to the question 'Who or what speaks?' that it is the dialectic and that this is not an instrument of knowledge but a dialectic of things themselves. If the sentence as published does represent Hyppolite's original intentions – and the same wording is retained in another slightly later posthumous collection[13] – his point would seem to be that *logos* or language (philosophical language being the topic of the paper) cannot be identified with absolute difference, because the latter is a function of the former; somewhat as a property of a thing cannot be all there is to that thing. Thus understood,

10   *Derrida on the Threshold of Sense*

Hyppolite would be paraphrasing the statement reproduced above from the *Phenomenology of Spirit* that 'this category or *simple* unity of self-consciousness and being possesses difference *in itself*'. We may never know for sure what Hyppolite intended. We may have here a case of meaning lost beyond recovery.[14] We are inclined to say however that we could in principle find out at least whether there had been a *lapsus* by getting Macksey and Donato or someone else to dig out Hyppolite's manuscript and compare it with the typescript and the proofs. Derrida is inclined to say that this would not show that there is not here and everywhere, a dissemination, a loss of meaning which cannot be recovered by any amount of research. Successful searching for answers to empirical and in general 'ontic' questions about lost MSS and mislaid umbrellas does not guarantee success when we seek answers to 'ontological' questions like What is meaning? What is being? and, in the context of dialectical ontology, What is *Aufhebung*? In a style resembling Wittgenstein's reaction to the first and Heidegger's reaction to the second, Derrida remarks on the third of these questions:

> As soon as the ontological question (What's this? What is? What is the meaning of being? etc.) gets deployed according to the process and structure of *Aufhebung*, is con-founded with the absolute of *Aufhebung*, it can no longer be asked: What is *Aufhebung*? as one would ask: What is this or that? or What is the definition of such and such a particular concept? Being is *Aufhebung*. *Aufhebung* is being, not like a determinate state or like the determinable totality of what is, but as the 'active' essence which produces being. It cannot therefore be the *object* of any determinate question. We are unendingly referred in that direction, but this reference refers to nothing determinable. [*Glas* 42–3 (47)]

Similarly with the questions Derrida puts in 'La Différance' echoing these and Hyppolite's Who or what is speaking?: Who or what de(dif)fers? What is differance?

III   WHAT IS TRANSGRESSION?

As Derrida would ask, what goes on in Bataille's 'transgression' of Hegel, *qu'est-ce qui se passe* in this passage? Put baldly, what takes place is a move from a restricted to a general economy. What Bataille calls general economy connects with what Derrida, in 'La Différance', *Positions*, *La Dissémination* and elsewhere, calls the general text, and with what he calls generalised *Verstimmung* (off-tuning?) in a contribution to the colloquium provoked by his writings which was held at Cerisy in 1980. All three of these expressions, along with 'writing', 'dissemination' and many others on which Derrida rings the changes, are universal operators whose generality is so generous that it cannot be contained within a universal concept or the covers of a book, no matter how encyclopædic the book may be.

At the outset of Derrida's meditation on Bataille there is a hint that the treatment will neither cure nor kill. Recognising the importance which dissemination has in Derrida's scheme one might expect that if he entitles his essay on Bataille 'From restricted to general economy' he will be for Bataille rather than against. This would be to take too naive a view of deconstruction and of his deconstruction of Bataille in particular. For Derrida's subtitle is 'An Hegelianism without reservation'. Does that mean that Bataille follows Hegel up to a point but transgresses or dislocates him by moving from an anal economy of saving and thrift to an economy of prodigal spending, potlatch and waste? Or does it mean that Bataille's project for a general economy is unreservedly Hegelian? Which? Both? Neither? These questions are left undecided by Derrida's choosing as an exergue for his piece Bataille's statement 'He [Hegel] did not know to what extent he was right', '*il ne sut pas dans quelle mesure il avait raison*'. Does he underestimate or overestimate the scope of reason? Was he, Hegel, less right about its limits than he thought, or more? Was Bataille? Derrida says 'Bataille is less Hegelian than he thinks' [*ED* 405 (275)]. He says this because Bataille himself says transgression is within the domain of the Hegelian dialectic. Bataille forgets he has been arguing that *Aufhebung* is an operation of a slavish mentality which takes as its point of departure the prohibitions of the master and invests them with a fuller meaning on the way to fulfilment in absolute knowing. On this account, one not obviously in keeping with Hyppolite's, *Aufhebung* is an economy of reproduction restricted to market values in which meanings are circulated without in the long run any profit or loss. Transgression, on the other hand, is a 'sovereign operation' of a general economy which exceeds the opposition of master and slave. Bataille's sovereignty is not therefore to be confused with Hegel's mastery. For the semantic economy of the latter is overcome by the semantic economy of the victorious slave, but also preserved by it. The latter is the truth of the former and both function within the realm of knowledge and sense. Sovereignty [f. OF *soverain* f. LL SUPER-(*anus*-AN); -g- by assoc. *reign*] as Bataille writes of it is beyond the realm of sense, a procedure of *Ent-sinnung* or dis-semination which, in a way to be later explained, suspends all phenomenological suspension [*ED* 393 (268)]. A non-knowledge. A non-science. A non-sense. It is the outlawing of the law, the ruling out of rules, the interdiction [*interdire*: to disconcert, nonplus, bewilder, render speechless] of interdiction [interdict: authoritative prohibition]. It cannot therefore be on Derrida's parsing of it an *Aufhebung* of Hegel's difference. It can only be the differance of difference. Its eye, to employ one of Bataille's metaphors, turns in towards the blind spot on the retina of knowledge. 'Sovereignty is absolute when it absolves itself from every relation and remains in the night of the secret. The *continuum* of sovereign communication has as its element this night of secret difference' [*ED* 391 (266)].

Yet although this transgressive operation of sovereignty is differance, not an *Aufhebung* of Hegelian difference, it is, Derrida adds

> powerless to transfrom the core (*noyau*) of predicates. Every attribute applied to sovereignty is borrowed from the (Hegelian) logic of mastery. We cannot, and Bataille could and should not dispose of any other concept or any other sign, of any other union of word and meaning. In its opposition to servility the sign 'sovereign' has already issued from the same mould as that of mastery.

On the scale of continuity-discontinuity Bataille's transgression and Derrida's displacement are somewhere between a Hegelian transmissive *Aufhebung* and a Bachelardian or Kuhnian intermissive break (*coupure*).[15]

But Bataille does not know to what degree he is right. He thinks he is more Hegelian than is in fact the case. Sometimes his thought follows extremely Hegelian lines, as Derrida brings out. 'One could even abstract in Bataille's text an entire zone which encircles sovereignty within a classic philosophy of the *subject* and above all within that *voluntarism* Heidegger has shown to have been con-founded by Hegel and Nietzsche with the essence of metaphysics' [*ED* 391–2 (267)]. However, if we are to have Bataille's general text to read, the warp of this line of thought must be unpicked and rewoven with a very un-Hegelian weft. So Derrida puts out a sobering reminder that sovereignty comes from the same mould as mastery and that Bataille's so-called gnostic materialism, like any other attempt to displace the oppositions of classical philosophy, like Derrida's own ('differance remains a metaphysical name' [*M* 28 (26)]), depend on that philosophy (is *parasitic* upon it? We come to that topic in Chapter 5). Even so, he cites from Bataille some sentences in which transgression is transgressed to the brink of a Bachelardian break.

> And it is not enough to say that one cannot speak about the sovereign moment without altering it, without altering it in respect of its true sovereignty. No less contradictory than speaking of it is trying to track down its movements. The moment we search for something, whatever it may be, we do not live sovereignly; we subordinate the present moment to a future one which will succeed it. We shall perhaps achieve the sovereign moment following our effort and it is indeed possible that an effort is necessary, but between the time of the effort and the sovereign time there is inevitably a break (*coupure*), one could even say an abyss. [*ED* 392 (336)]

How we see the relation between Bataille's transgression, Hegel's *Aufhebung*, Derrida's displacement and Bachelard's break will depend in part of course on our reading of Hegel's doctrine of difference. We saw that Hyppolite's reading of this assimilates it towards the inklings we are coming to have of Derridian differance and displacement. Derrida gives two readings of Hegel, or perhaps we should say a double reading. Where he is describing Bataille's 'Hegelianism without reservation' he notes that Bataille describes himself as a Hegelian. Derrida also notes how misleading this is. In explaining why this is so he gives a more conservative reading of Hegel's doctrine of difference than does Hyppolite, and he assimilates Bataille's transgression to Derridian differance and displacement. Elsewhere his reading is more unreservedly like that given by Hyppolite. There is a hint of such a reading in 'Le Puits et la pyramide' the first version of which was presented at Hyppolite's seminar at the Collège de France in January 1968. He cites some sentences from the end of a Remark in the *Science of Logic* on 'The employment of numerical distinctions for expressing philosophical concepts':

> Calculation being so much an external and therefore mechanical business, it has been possible to construct machines which perform mathematical operations with complete accuracy. A knowledge of just this one fact about the nature of calculation is sufficient for an appraisal of the idea of making calculation the principal means for educating the mind and stretching it on the rack in order to perfect it as a machine.

Derrida comments on the irony of these sentences. It is with more irony that he suggests they may be made – though not without more stretching on the rack – to cough up that 'secret difference' of the dead loss no name can name, no sign can signify and no dialectical breath of life can remedy. Hegel would be the last to confess such an eldritch secret. But Derrida diagnoses symptoms of dis-ease in what he takes to be non-dialectical contradictions, unresolvable inconsistencies, in certain of Hegel's pronouncements about mathematical abstraction, formalistic understanding and the priority of speech over writing. For example, Hegel maintains that the Chinese epoch is one in which formalism and mathematics predominate. Since he says these as well as the degree of grammatical development and differentiatedness of a language are functions of the understanding, one would expect the grammar of Chinese to be highly differentiated. But Hegel denies that it is. On the other hand, he does claim that Chinese lexicology is very rich. He says this too of German which he therefore considers spiritually and philosophically advanced. Yet the Chinese moment of cultural history, in spite of the abundance of its lexicology, he deems spiritually and philosophically retarded.

Other sentences in which Hegel expresses his low opinion of Chinese hieroglyphism and of non-phonetic writing in general are quoted in the early part of *De la grammatologie* which may be regarded, Derrida mentions, as a development of a paper published in December 1965 and January 1966, that is, six or seven months before Hyppolite's Baltimore paper was tabled. Despite the higher estimation of speaking compared with writing which is manifest *passim* by the author of the books we know as the *Encyclopædia* and the *Science of Logic*, everything Hegel has thought within the horizon of the metaphysics of propriety, Derrida concedes, everything except the eschatology

> can be read as a meditation on writing. Hegel is *also* the thinker of irreducible difference. He has rehabilitated thinking as productive memory of signs. And he has reintroduced . . . the essential necessity of the written trace into a philosophical – i.e. Socratic – discourse which had always believed it could manage without it: the last philosopher of the book and the first thinker of writing. [*G* 41 (26)]

If Bataille and Derrida are on the threshold, Hegel is only slightly preliminary. Although he remains the *thinker* of writing, he is on the way to a deconstruction of the opposition between explicitation and the clean break, between smooth continuity and sudden discontinuity [*Glas* 123–4 (150–1)], a displacement of displacement which shows that although Hegel is said to be the last philosopher of the book and the first thinker of writing, and although the chapter where this is said is entitled 'The End of the Book and the beginning of writing', the book has no end and there is no beginning of writing [*Pos* 23 (14)].

Hegel is only slightly preliminary only if exception is made for his eschatology. In the foursome with Bachelard and Bataille, Hegel and Derrida do not see eye to eye where what is in question is the teleology of absolute knowing. Here their vis-à-vis becomes a dos-à-dos. The teleology of absolute knowing is a doctrine of possible presence. If Derrida is unwilling to go along with that doctrine he can be expected to be out of step also with Husserl, for Husserl's non-dialectical phenomenology is a doctrine of presence, *parousia*. That Husserl is both at home and not at home in this doctrine is one of the lessons of Derrida's *Speech and Phenomena* and of his introduction to a translation of Husserl's *Origin of Geometry*, as we shall now see.

2 Transcendental Phenomenological Semiology

> The most important lesson which the reduction teaches us is the impossibility of a complete reduction.
>
> Maurice Merleau-Ponty

I HUSSERL AND THE PRESENCE OF BRENTANO

In 1904–5, that *annus mirabilis* for theories of time, in lectures edited by Heidegger in 1928, Husserl prepares the way for Heidegger's demonstration in 1927 that the Aristotelian atomic Now is parasitic upon the diasporatic *Augenblick*, the moment of vision with its Janus characteristic of looking fore and aft. It is not directly Aristotle's account of time however but Brentano's which is singled out for criticism in the *Lectures on the Phenomenology of Internal Time Consciousness*. That account is cast in terms of 'contents' and is largely psychologistic. Like Hume, according to Husserl, Brentano never gets a firm hold on the difference between psychology and phenomenology. Another weakness Husserl finds is that Brentano limits his account to the temporality of the content of apprehension, ignoring the temporality of the act, thereby throwing away any chance of anticipating Husserl's own distinctions between noetic act, noematic *Objekt* and real *Gegenstand*. More seriously erroneous in Husserl's opinion is Brentano's attribution of our ideas of the past and future to the productive imagination. When we listen to a melody we are presented with a content which is the sound of the note being struck now. If we are to grasp the melodic line it is not sufficient that the sound be retained. That would give us at most the experience of a chord. We must have the idea of one sound

16

succeeding another, of one being past and of others to come. Brentano sees that attempts to explain the origin of our ideas of pastness and future in terms of the character of the physical stimulus or in terms of the duration or succession of a mental act beg the question and confuse the sensation of duration and succession with the duration and succession of sensations. His solution is to propose what he calls a primordial sensation in which a sensation gives rise to a similar idea with a new temporal character of pastness, this latter giving rise in the imagination to yet another temporally modified idea, and so on. His account of our anticipations of perception takes its cue from Hume's reference to the creation in imagination of an idea of a colour shade of which we have never had an impression. The idea of the future is formed by extrapolation from our idea of the past. As a corollary of this Brentano asserts that only the Now is real, other temporal predicates being non-real (*irreale*).

Husserl's chief reason for rejecting Brentano's theory is that by restricting the perception of temporality to the boundary between the past and the future he renders himself incapable of accommodating the phenomenological difference between (re)presentation and 'presentification' (*Vergegenwärtigung*), that is, the representation of (re)presentation. It is not enough for Brentano to say that my reproduction in imagination today of a melodic sequence I heard yesterday is the auditory imaging of an auditory imaging. This misses the experiential difference between two sorts of memory, viz. retention and reproduction. There is 'a radical difference in content'.[1] Husserl suggests that to appreciate this we need only compare what Brentano might call the after-image of a sound with a reproduction of that after-image while the original sound is still ringing in our ears.

So Husserl concludes not only that 'a punctual phase can never be for itself'.[2] Brentano would accept that. He concludes also, against Brentano, that 'the whole sphere of primordial associations is a present and real lived experience'.[3] It is this second conclusion that Derrida 'deconstructs', exposing a strain between it and the account of retentions and protentions heralded in the first.

Before enquiring into what Derrida discovers in this quarter of Husserl's text it should be observed that there are grounds for expecting that if Husserl is found to have a weakness there he will be found to have one in other quarters too. For Husserl maintains there is an analogy between the way my past is given to me and the way other egos are appresented. In the *Lectures* he writes:

> Just as in perception I see what has being now, and in extended perceptions, no matter how constituted, what has enduring being, so in primary remembrance I see what is past. What is past is given therein, and givenness of the past is memory.[4]

Later, in the *Cartesian Meditations*, he adds:

> Just as, in my living present, in the domain of 'internal perception', my past becomes constituted by virtue of the harmonious memories occurring in this present, so in my primordial sphere, by means of appresentations occurring in it and motivated by its contents, an ego other than mine can become constituted – accordingly in non-originary presentations (*Vergegenwärtigungen*) of a new type, which have a modification of a new kind as their correlate.[5]

'In both cases', Husserl notes, 'the modification is inherent as a sense-component in the sense itself.' And there is a third case of which this must be said, that of the appresented aspects of a presented thing, its 'possible perceptions'. These are but three cases of what Husserl calls transcendence. Yet that is one of the words Derrida uses for what he claims Husserl too frequently forgets. And there is a fourth dimension of transcendence which Derrida acknowledges in Husserl, that of the Idea taken in a Kantian sense. This has an important role in *Ideas* and subsequent writings of Husserl. In the detailed introduction to his translation of the *Origin of Geometry* Derrida teases out the implications for phenomenology of Husserl's recourse to the Idea. In the *Cartesian Meditations* Husserl stresses that evidence can be apodictic without being adequate. This possibility is shown by the fact that any physical thing has an infinity of unperceived aspects and yet, says Husserl, it is apodictically evident that this is so. One challenge to this is forestalled by the distinction Husserl, like Locke, makes between an idea of infinity and an infinite idea.[6] That distinction does not however resolve the difficulty Derrida finds lurking behind all of these admissions of transcendence. In spite of these admissions, Derrida says, Husserl vacillates and is not sufficiently radical.

Derrida traces this failure of nerve back to the theory of meaning and expression which Husserl begins to develop in the First and Sixth Investigation and continues in *Ideas* and in *Formal and Transcendental Logic*.

II DERRIDA AND THE PRESENCE OF HUSSERL

Husserlian transcendental phenomenology performs a series of 'reductions' which, somewhat after the manner of Cartesian methodological doubt, suspend all questions of contingent existence with a view to describing the residual essential structures of meaning or sense. For these meanings or senses which phenomenology describes Husserl uses the word *Sinn*. He notes that the word *Bedeutung* is commonly used coterminously with *Sinn* and states that he will follow that usage. He proposes to favour the words *Bedeutung* and *bedeuten* however when talking of what he calls specifically logical or expressive meaning. 'Logical meaning (*Bedeutung*) is expression (*Ausdruck*)',[7] he says, and only voluntary expression is here intended, not involuntary facial expression, intonation or gesture.[8] As long as the picture is not taken too seriously, he goes on, we may regard expression as a stratum laid over the pre-expressive substratum of noematic sense. Thus to mean something expressly will be to intend an ideal ob-jective noematic sense which has been raised to the level of the logical, the conceptual and the general.

It is important to note that according to Husserl this raising need not involve physical marks or sounds. If it did the reduced world of phenomenology would risk pollution by the physical. Expressive meanings (*Bedeutungen*) are ideal objects and these must not be confused with real (*real*) things existing in space and time, that is *Gegenstände*. Nor must they be confused with the parallel and no less real psychological realm. To make the former confusion would be to run the risk of erring in the direction of materialism and realism. To make the second would be to be in danger of subjective idealism and the psychologism criticised at length in the Prolegomena of the *Logical Investigations*.

Husserl therefore sharply distinguishes expressive intention (*Hinzeigen*) from indication (*Anzeigen*). What is indicated is not fully present to me. When for instance someone is saying something with the intention of pointing out to me (*hinweisen*) that it is going to rain or that a certain conclusion follows from certain premisses (*beweisen*), I gather (*kundnehmen*) what he intends without his intention being manifest to me in the manner in which what I intend is manifest to me. His saying what he says only gives me to understand what he intends (*kundgeben*). Indication is bracketed off along with reference to particular things, so that there is left in the field of expression only ideal meanings and ideal word types. The type is the spiritual body of meaning. It is a purely expressive sign whose indicative function comes into play, Husserl says, only where expressions are being used communicatively. But there is no effective communication with the words and the meanings as these are studied phenomenologically. It is only a *façon de parler* to hold that within the phenomenological reduction the soul speaks indicatively to itself. Because in such monologue it is in immediate presence to itself, indicative signs are superfluous. I can have only an imaginary conversation with myself. As Husserl puts it, imagination or fiction is 'the element which makes up the life of phenomenology'.[9] This should not hide from us however that the essential insight which phenomenology seeks is '*a primordial dator act, and as such analogous to perception, and not to imagination*'.[10] This is what Husserl calls the principle of all principles. It is on account of this principle that Derrida points out that 'even if it is a good auxiliary instrument of phenomenological neutralization, the image is not a pure neutralization. It retains a primary reference to a primordial presentation, that is, to a perception and positing of existence, to a belief in general' [*VP* 62 (55)].

Derrida also points out that although the imaginary conversations of the phenomenologist with himself may appear to have no place for indication, imagined indication involves real indication through the very fact that it involves signs. For the ideal represented (*vorgestellte*) sign in its role as representative or delegate standing for something has not only a vertical expressive relation with the idea it stands for; it also has a horizontal alterity of non-presence in that its ideality implies repeatability. Its typicality is the plurality of its tokens. Whether it be a question of the ideality of the signifier or of the ideality of the signified, 'Absolute ideality is the correlate of a possibility of indefinite repetition' [*VP* 58 (52)].

Husserl affirms:

No theory we can conceive can mislead us in regard to the *principle of all principles*: that *every primordial dator Intuition is a source of authority (Rechtsquelle)* for knowledge, that *whatever presents itself in 'intuition' in primordial form* (as it were in its bodily reality) *is simply to be accepted as it gives itself out to be, though only within the limits in which it then presents itself.* Let our insight grasp this fact that the theory itself in turn could not derive its truth except from primordial data. Every statement which does nothing more than give expression to such data through merely unfolding their meaning and adjusting it accurately is thus really . . . an absolute beginning, called in a genuine sense to provide foundations, a *principium*.[11]

This principle of all principles states that knowledge of principles is based on intuition of essences. It is therefore not only about the ideal object seen but also about the seeing of it by a subject who comes to see it at a particular moment. This moment of vision and moment of truth is a moment in which the truth has to be represented (*vorgestellt*) by a transcendental subject. Husserl conceives this representation as an immediate presence in the present. That explains why he wishes to make do with purely expressive signification.

It also explains why he later comes to speak of expression as though it were independent of signs, the word 'sign' now being reserved for indication. Derrida draws attention to Husserl's use in the First Investigation of the phrase '. . . as signs, i.e. as indications . . . (. . . *als Zeichen, nämlich als Anzeichen* . . .)'. He rightly refuses to regard this itself as sufficient evidence of a departure from Husserl's initial division of signs into the expressive and the indicative, for Husserl's sentence is 'Shall one say that in soliloquy one speaks to oneself, and employs words as signs, i.e. as indications, of one's own inner experiences?'[12] Here 'i.e.' translates a *nämlich* which is specificatory rather than appositional, as the rest of the paragraph confirms. Derrida puts more weight on Husserl's remark in *Ideas* that 'The thing that appears to sense, which has the sensory properties of shape, colour, smell, and taste, is therefore far from being a sign for *something else*, though to a certain extent a sign *for itself*'.[13] In the paragraphs leading up to this sentence Husserl has been arguing against the representative realist theory that the physicist has direct knowledge only of appearances, not of the causes of appearances. In the paragraphs following the quoted sentence Husserl makes it clear that what he means in saying that a sensible thing is a sign for itself is that a given sensible property, e.g. the shape or the colour, may be an indicator of ungiven sensible properties, e.g. the smell or the taste. In other words he is endorsing that part of Locke's theory according to which some properties – and according to Locke 'a great part of our complex ideas of substance' — are synechdochic 'retainers' to others.[14] Although this is reasonable and right, it cannot be used to prop up Derrida's assertion that, since being a sign of itself is tantamount to not being a sign, Husserl is here tacitly denying that there is signification in the moment of vision (*Augenblick*), that is to say, in the moment of 'primordial data consciousness' [*VP* 68 (61)].[15]

Husserl is also right, in the various statements Derrida cites in the same connection from the Sixth Investigation, the *Lectures* and *Ideas*, to draw attention to the difference in phenomenological experience between perception or intuition on the one hand and the symbolic representation by means of images or signs on the other.[16] But, as Derrida notes, Husserl overlooks a logical similarity and is inconsistent with himself in doing so. As regards the first oversight, it is manifest from the principle of principles and what Husserl says about it that he is dealing with eidetic knowledge. Such knowledge presupposes not just an experience in the sense of something lived through (*erlebt*). It presupposes an ob-ject which is known and the perception or intuition in which someone sees that it is a necessary truth and hence that registration of it is in principle repeatable *ad infinitum*. Husserl himself says that ideality is omnitemporality. But how, he asks in the *Origin of Geometry*, can the ideal truths of, for instance, geometry get beyond the merely personal evidence they have for their inventor and beyond the merely personal evidence which they have in the community of the original inventor and those who speak with him, to the objectivity and '*persisting existence* of "ideal objects" even during periods in which the inventor and his fellows are no longer wakefully so related or even are no longer alive'?[17] The answer Husserl gives to this question is that it is by writing that this objectivity is facilitated – and that this very facility is a source of 'the crisis in European sciences'.

This answer is the thread which Derrida follows through the

labyrinth of Husserl's phenomenological semiology to show that this semiology is in contradiction with itself. For that semiology invokes the possibility of an intuitive living self-presence such as would be achieved fully, if it is capable of being achieved at all, in the assertion 'I am' or 'I am alive'. But the possibility of my death and de-presence is written into the possibility of my saying that I am alive. Token reflexives, which Husserl calls essentially occasional expressions, are not logically proper names. What they express is universal. So what I express when I say 'I am' or 'I am alive' retains its meaning even when its object, which in this case is the subject making the statement, is dead. The same holds for first personal judgements of perception, for expressions of hope, doubt, desire or fear, etc., and for statements incorporating definite descriptions, for example 'The present Kaiser of Germany is bald'.[18]

In the *Phenomenology of Spirit* Hegel writes:

> when I say 'I', this singular 'I', I say in general all 'Is'; everyone is what I say, everyone is 'I', this singular 'I'. When Science is faced with the demand – as if it were an acid test it could not pass – that it should deduce, construct, find *a priori*, or however it is put, something called 'this thing' or 'this one man', it is reasonable that the demand should *say (sage)* which 'this thing', or which 'this particular man' is *meant (meine)*, but it is impossible to say this.[19]

It is perhaps with these remarks ringing in his ears that Derrida asserts that Husserl should hold that *'I am immortal* is an impossible proposition' [*VP* 61 (54)]. Admittedly, this allegedly impossible proposition is *prima facie* of a different class from that to which belong the propositions of which Husserl says his principle of all principles 'holds in special measure', namely, propositions which are essential and general in intent (*Meinung*). But even if it is not of the same class as these, the phrase 'in special measure' allows that it could still fall within the scope of the principle of all principles. In any case, this principle holds that principles which are explicitly essential and universal in form and intent are founded on intuitions which are expressed in first personal judgements of perception, and the first person pronouns which these require have the universality to which Hegel and Derrida advert. This universality, Husserl and Derrida agree, is graphically illustrated by the written sign. The written statement is typically testamentary, continuing to perform its function in spite of the absence and death of its author. The 'I' of 'I am writing' is anonymous and improper. But so too is the 'I' of 'I am speaking', though Husserl does not acknowledge this, for he wants to construe this 'I' as a logically proper name.

In support of his statement that there is a strain here in Husserl's texts Derrida refers to passages in the *Formal and Transcendental Logic* which are foreshadowed in the *Logical Investigations* where Husserl insists that pure logical grammar requires that a claim to perceive a particular thing like a golden mountain can be understood even if there is no such thing there to be perceived. As Derrida remarks, it is therefore surprising that Husserl does not say something analogous of statements embodying token reflexives, that although he allows that the absence of a golden mountain does not affect the meaningfulness of a statement using the phrase 'golden mountain', he does not allow that a statement like 'I am alive' can be meaningful if the author of it is unidentified or dead.

Husserl says: 'If we read this word ['I'] without knowing who wrote it, it is perhaps not meaningless (*bedeutungslos*) but it is at least estranged from its normal meaning.' Derrida's comment on this is that 'Husserl's premisses should sanction our saying exactly the contrary' [*VP* 107 (96)]. One premiss Derrida has in mind is conveyed in Husserl's assertion that in a judgement of perception such as 'I see a golden mountain' and 'I see a round square' a distinction must be made between content and object, where by 'content' is understood the self-identical meaning that the hearer can grasp even if he does not see what is said to be there or if there is nothing there of the kind described for anyone to perceive.[20] Just as it is structurally implied that the statement has meaning in these circumstances, so, Derrida says, 'we understand the word *I* not only when its "author" is unknown but when he is quite fictitious. And when he is dead'. In these circumstances the word has its *normal* meaning. We return in a later chapter to what he says about the normal, about authority and about fiction. We shall comment now only on what he says about death and the 'impossibility' of 'I am immortal'.

In saying that Husserl should hold that this proposition is impossible Derrida does not mean that he should say that it is nonsensical (*unsinnig*) or without sense (*sinnlos* or *bedeutungslos*).

He means that he should say that it is false because countersensical (*widersinnig*) or contradictory. It is not however directly contradictory in the manner of a proposition which both affirms and denies that I am immortal. Derrida is saying, if I understand him aright, that on Husserl's terms the proposition is indirectly contradictory or self-stultifying because it affirms that I am immortal, whereas Husserl's pure logical grammar entails that 'My death is structurally necessary to the pronouncing of the *I*', or, as Derrida also puts it, that my statement is accompanied by my being dead. Derrida realises that this latter way of putting the point may conjure up weird ideas of the sort one might encounter in stories by Poe, one of which, incidentally, is cited as a frontispiece to *Speech and Phenomena* and another of which is alluded to frequently in later publications including *La Carte postale* to which we shall allude in a later chapter. He therefore assures us at once that he means nothing more mysterious than the perfectly ordinary fact about speaking that the possibility of any first personal singular statement requires the possibility that I be dead. Why, we may ask, should this mean that 'I am immortal', in contrast to 'I am alive', be contradictory and therefore false? Why could it not be true that I am immortal and yet possible, though counterfactually, that I be dead? Won't a counterfactual possibility do to meet the rule of pure logical grammar that propositions are bipolar, that is, that what is true must conceivably be false, and vice-versa? Derrida's reply would be that if we think this is all that is needed we are either forgetting that he is concerned with the status of 'I am immortal' within Husserl's theory of meaning and expression or forgetting that this theory aims to bracket off all matters of particular fact. It must consequently have nothing to do with *la mienne*, that is, with the particular intent or meaning that is mine for which Hegel employs the word *Meinung* with an intended pun. A phenomenological semiology purports to limit itself to an original transcendental universal living presence. Now 'To think presence as a universal form of transcendental life is to open myself to the knowledge that in my absence, beyond my empirical existence, before my birth and after my death, *the present is*'. Hence in the phenomenological living present 'I' has its universal meaning and 'I am' has a presence in general as its meaning. This phenomenon of presence in general depends on the general idea of my possible disappearance. In the field of original living

presence 'I am' means 'I am present' and 'I am present' implies
that I might be absent and that I am mortal, that is, I could
conceivably die – not that I empirically will die, for we have
bracketed off all matters of empirical fact.

Hence, whatever may be the case in the suspended real world
of facts about which we make communications, within the
transcendental field of living presence 'I am immortal' is unthinkable. Within this field 'I am mortal' and 'I am immortal'
lack the bipolar symmetry of ordinary factual assertions and
their denials and the asymmetry they have there is not of the kind
which might be attributed to the statements 'I am mortal' and 'I
am immortal' on the grounds that the former is empirically
verifiable but not empirically falsifiable whereas the latter is
empirically falsifiable though not empirically verifiable.

What Derrida hopes this discussion of Husserl's theory of
token reflexivity will bring to our notice is something that
escapes the notice of Husserl himself: that the supposedly immaculate interiority of allegedly purely expressive meaning is
hymeneally conjugated with the exteriority of indication. This
exteriority is not simply appended to expressive meaning. It is
already inscribed within its threshold. Its supplementation is not
an additive and adulterative ingression; it is a complementation
in the sense that there is no expressive meaning without indication. Indication and expressive meaning do not lie alongside
each other in the manner of the parallelism Husserl posits
between psychology and phenomenology. There is a mutual
completion and inextricable interference which Derrida likens to
the crossing over of the chiasmus. What looks like a limit
between them is de-limited. Expressive meaning is already disseminated. Where, as in Hegel, 'writing' stands for spatialising
alterity and 'speech' for temporal presence, writing, Derrida
says, does not sidle up to speech. It has already double-crossed
it. It is what animates and arouses it: 'elle l'a doublée en
l'animant dès son éveil'. This shows how complete the double-
crossing is. We are used to the idea that meaning animates the
indicative sign, as the soul gives the breath of life to the body.
But, as Saussure already recognises [*Pos* 28 (18)], this is too
simple-minded an analogy. Derrida is saying that the life of the
indicative sign gives life to expressive meaning. The intimacy of
signifier and signified conception is such that not only can there
be no meaning without indicative signifier; the body of the sign,

the signifier, is already spiritualised, so to speak, i.e. eternalised or, to use Husserl's word, omnitemporalised, by its essential repeatability. The mortality of the sensible corporeal token puts on the immortality of the infinite iterability of the type without which and, since the type is the type of a token, with which there can be no *soi-disant* immortal consciousness of sense [*VP* 61 (54–5)]. Here we see how Derrida's deconstruction of Husserl's phenomenological semiology has two stages. In the first stage the order of priority is reversed: 'Here indication does not degrade expression or lead it astray; it dictates it.' But this reversal which appears to confer dictatorial superiority on the hitherto subordinated term of the contrasted pair is succeeded in due course by a second stage, which it is tempting but quite misleading to think of as a stage at which there is a synthesis of a thesis and an antithesis, where there is no question of deciding an order of priority and where one does not and cannot in principle know what to say. Why this should be so will gradually become clearer, it is hoped, as further specimens of Derridian deconstruction are worked through in the pages of this book. Anyone who, having traversed its pages so far, feels that an embargo is laid on clarity by Derrida's resorting to the metaphors of body and soul, life and death, etc., instead of restricting himself to the literal language of tokens, types, sense and reference, may be motivated to read the rest of them by the thought that it will be learned from them why one of the oppositions Derrida deconstructs is this very one between literality and metaphor. Nevertheless some clarification will be attempted immediately of what Derrida and Husserl mean by reference and indication.

III   REFERENCE AND INDICATION

J. N. Mohanty believes that Derrida confuses reference and indication whereas Husserl distinguishes them.[21] His argument to this effect is important because it compels us to recognise that Derrida interprets the *Logical Investigations* very much in the light of Husserl's later more articulated phenomenology. Derrida himself argues that Husserl is anticipating the method of transcendental phenomenological reduction when he says in the *Logical Investigations* that indication is suspended in soliloquy. Mohanty makes the perfectly fair comment that in ordinary soliloquy reference is not suspended, hence reference cannot be the same as indication. Less fair, I believe, is his comment on Derrida's statement that 'indicative significations in language will cover everything that falls subject to the "reductions"; factuality, worldly existence, essential non-necessity, non-evidence, etc.' He rejects this on the grounds that as well as indicating worldly existence one can refer to it. This objection does not seem to me to be valid. Everything we can refer to may be something we can also indicate. However that leaves us with a difference between reference and indication, the difference that, according to Mohanty, Husserl observes and Derrida obscures. I have conceded that there can be reference in ordinary 'inner speech' (soliloquy). I think that Husserl would allow this although he denies that in ordinary inner speech there can be indication. It seems to me however that he denies that there is reference to factual existents or non-existents in fully reduced phenomenological inner speech. Just as he can allow that there are indicative *expressions* in ordinary inner speech which do not function as such, so he can allow that there are referring *expressions* in phenomenologically reduced speech, but he must deny that they are there used to refer to factual existents. (Indicative and referring *expressions* are of course not to be confused with expressive *meaning*.)

Mohanty's disagreement with Derrida is explained by their each concentrating on different senses of reference and indication to be found in Husserl's text. Mohanty cites Husserl's remark: 'To use an expression significantly and to refer (*se rapporter* in the translation Derrida uses) expressively to an object – to form a presentation of it (*se représenter l'objet*) – are one and the same'.[22] He cites this in support of his own statement that according to Husserl 'The referring function is thus not contingent to an expression'. This statement is verbally identical with what I am saying Derrida believes Husserl fails to acknowledge. No more than verbally however. In the remark Mohanty cites Husserl is making the point he has previously made in section 13 of the *Logical Investigations*. In the English translation that section bears the title 'Connection between meaning and objective reference'. The phrase 'objective reference' here translates *Beziehung* and the thesis of the section could be put in traditional terminology by saying that the connotation of an expression fixes its denotation. This is a thesis about expressions, whether or not they are referring expressions in the narrower sense I am saying Derrida is in fact concerned with when he makes his statement about Husserl's oversight. In making this he uses Husserl's word 'indication', but the indicative expressions in Husserl which he has in mind are, as we have seen, Husserl's 'essentially occasional' expressions. These include 'I', 'this' and nouns used with the definite article as in phrases like 'the Kaiser'. In the sense in which these expressions are typically used to refer Derrida's view is that Husserl fails to acknowledge the fact that even under the conditions of transcendental phenomenological reduction expressive meaning is dependent on reference.

IV *TELOS* AND *EIDOS*

Husserl says 'There are objects – and all transcendent objects, all "realities" (*Realitäten*) which are included under the rubric Nature or World are here included – which cannot be given with complete determinacy and with similarly complete intuitability in any finite consciousness'.[23] The words 'There are objects' with which this assertion begins suggest that some objects can be completely given, and we saw at the end of the first section of this chapter that Husserl defends the right to say that the Idea, in a Kantian sense, of an asymptotic approach to the complete givenness of a physical thing and (as he says in section 83 of *Ideas* I) of a stream of experience, can be itself given apodictically. In the Introduction to *Ideas* I he mentions the misinterpretations of the terms 'Idea' and 'Ideal' proposed by readers of the *Logical Investigations*. When he writes that the idea of an uncompleted progression is given apodictically the word 'Idea' is being used for the proposition, principle or truth that, in words of his own which anticipate a controversy over phenomenalism, 'The "and so forth" is an absolutely indispensable phase in the thing-noema'.[24] Rather as the discussions about innate ideas since the seventeenth century have tended to become discussions about principles, so Husserl's discussion of meaning turns into talk of truth. This is most obviously so where he is occupied with the objectivity of the sciences and of mathematics in particular. And it is in this last field, if anywhere, that we should expect fulfilment to be really full. Derrida holds that in Husserl's view even in this field complete fulfilment is not in fact achieved, but is only a *telos*. Even in mathematics, Husserl says in the *Origin of Geometry*, 'Ultimately, objective, absolutely firm knowledge of truth is an infinite idea'.[25] As with Plato, from whom Kant himself says he derives his notion of an Idea of Reason, the *eidos* is a value, so with Husserl, who acknowledges his indebtedness to Kant, the idea is an ideal, or at least it becomes an ideal when it comes to be treated as a truth. Perhaps when it does come to be treated as a truth its teleologicality is not in conflict with the statement in the First Investigation that the ideality of meaning (*Bedeutung*) is not ideality in a normative sense, by which Husserl means that it has the ideality of a species, not the ideality of an individual, that is, not the normative ideality a traditional Platonist realism ascribes to exemplary Ideas. Yet of the expression of meanings even in mathematical formulæ Husserl is apparently prepared to say what he says, in a passage Derrida quotes from the First Investigation, of any statements incorporating token reflexives:

> But what is objectively quite definite must permit objective determination, and what permits objective determination must, ideally speaking, permit expression through wholly determinate word-meanings . . . . We are infinitely remote from this ideal . . . .[26]

Other reasons why Husserl thinks the ideal of scientific objectivity to be infinitely remote are spelled out in the *Origin of Geometry*. Although the objectivity of science demands written as well as spoken language, this objectivity is put at risk by that very fact. Succumbing to the 'seductions of language', we 'lapse into a kind of talking and reading that is dominated purely by association'.[27] Moreover, although the chains of premises in the deductive sciences increase in length and complexity over the centuries, it exceeds the mathematician's finite capacity to reactivate the original insights in a unitary survey, to make them his own, to give them authority and authenticity (*Eigentlichkeit*).[28] That ideal survey *sub specie æternitatis* has therefore to be put off to infinity. We have to put up with the pro-visional. Disappointed of presence in the present, Husserl postpones it. But his hankering after this *summum verum* derives from his will to obey what Derrida calls the intuitionistic imperative of the principle of all principles [*VP* 109 (97)]. We saw that in his statement of this principle he writes of '*an absolute beginning* . . . foundations, a *principium*'. According to Derrida such an absolute beginning is a myth which does not cease being a myth when archæology makes way for eschatology and the absolute origin is converted into an absolute end. This myth is already at work in Plato's *Phædrus* where, when the invention of writing is being discussed, Socrates rejects the suggestion that the invention is an aid to memory on the grounds that it is not anamnetic but at best mechanically mnemonic and hypomnetic. This putative remedy, *pharmakon*, does more harm than good, for it introduces a poison, *pharmakon*, into the well-spring of truth by creating a space between the soul and its dialogue with itself. This Socratic picture of self-presence in inner speech is an ancestor *via* Descartes of the Husserlian image of the living present of the meditating philosopher's self-communing in phenomenological *viva voce* where questions contain their answers,[29] where to understand (*entendre*) is to hear, to hear (*entendre*) is to understand, and where the phoneme presents itself as the mastered ideality of the phenomenon [*VP* 78 (87)].

But Husserl's metaphysical nostalgia for univocal self-identical presence is accompanied by an acknowledgement of the inescapability of at least the four kinds of differentiating elsewhereness mentioned in the first section of this chapter (elsewhereness of retention and protention, of the other's consciousness, of possible perceptions, and of the Idea in a Kantian sense), by the largely unacknowledged commitment to non-presence of the kind discussed in the second section, and by the acknowledgement noticed in this final section that the presence of meaning is infinitely deferred. This amounts to an acknowledgement of defeat for the theories of phenomenological semiology and pure logical grammar. The principles of these theories, like those of any other, must obey the intuitionistic imperative of the principle of all principles. Fulfilment by the presentations of intuitive dator consciousness is a condition of their apodicticity. If presentation is depresented through postponement to infinity, this condition cannot be fulfilled.

3   Fundamental Ontological Semiology

Philosophy is properly nostalgia – the aspiration to be *at home everywhere*.

Novalis, *Encyclopædia*

I   WHAT IS THE SENSE OF BEING?

It has been shown in Chapters 1 and 2 that, according to Derrida, Hegel and Husserl turn themselves inside out to found their philosophies on two incompatible principles, a principle of presence and a principle of non-presence. It might be supposed that no such reading of Heidegger would be possible, for in *Being and Time* he, as he puts it, 'destroys' the metaphysics of presence which he maintains is subscribed to by Hegel and Husserl and the metaphysical tradition as a whole. For instance, although he rarely mentions Husserl by name, he holds that phenomenological ontology founded on his principle of all principles is not really fundamental. To start with, it is too narrow. It studies being in terms of consciousness of noematic objects, but this is not the only mode of being. In so far as it attempts to think ontologically it thinks being in terms of present at hand beings, data presented to an intuiting subject. Phenomenology, Heidegger says in the Introduction to *Being and Time*, must ask not only about the immediate data of consciousness. It must ask also after what conceals itself, the meaning of being, and it must try to bring out why this concealment takes place, why one forgets the ontological difference between being and beings. His own attempt to do this takes the form of a scrutiny of the texts of philosophy from its origins in Ancient Greece through to Nietzsche.

Derrida's programme has affinities with Heidegger's. It has its point of departure in the Heideggerian theme of ontological difference. He insists that one cannot get around Heidegger's ontological difference and that it has to be gone through; it is an ancestor of his own differance, and the task attempted by this latter could never have been envisaged without it [*Pos* 18 (9)]. This task, however, includes a demonstration that Heidegger's questioning of being is still tied to the metaphysics of presence and the principle of all principles even though the version of the principle to which he subscribes disclaims appeal to some sufficient present entity or Entity as ground. This adherence exceeds the adherence which Heidegger and Derrida admit to be inevitable because any project which deconstructs a system is bound to that system's language. It is an adherence which is not tactical or strategical but doctrinal. It manifests itself in the emphasis Heidegger puts upon proximity and propriety in his revision of the traditional conception of self-consciousness. This revision is cast in terms of being and being there, rather than consciousness, and it is preliminary to a questioning of the meaning of being which aims to free itself from onto-theology, that is, from ways of thinking dominated by the principle of sufficient reason and the ontic categories of substance and property. This ontology has an ontic point of departure. It begins with a being, a being whose being is to be (t)here, *Da-sein*, an existential way of being as opposed to the categorical ways of being of data and the tools with which we handle them. It begins there because that way of being is the way of human being and this is manifest in the entity that is closest to us, ourselves.

As well as this ontic proximity there is the ontological proximity, the nearness to this existent of being. This existent is and exists its being. Dasein is pre-ontologically, that is, pre-analytically and pre-theoretically, ontological, that is, familiar with being. But for reasons which it is one of the aims of *Being and Time* to make clear, Dasein's interpretations of itself tend to be in terms of the categories of the non-existential entities in the world. Heidegger believes that the history of philosophy shows that ontologically, in its accounts of being, Dasein is remote from being. *Being and Time* and Heidegger's later work undertake the destruction of these historical constructions, destruction being 'a critical process in which the traditional concepts, which at first must necessarily be employed, are de-constructed down to the sources from which they are drawn', this being the only way in which ontology can achieve a phenomenological attestation of its concepts.[1] A style of thinking has to be sought in which the gap between being and our concepts of being is closed.

Derrida cites many passages where this reminiscence of being is described as a bringing near. For example in the *Letter on Humanism* Heidegger writes of reaching a nearness to the truth, the disclosure (*aletheia*), of being [*M* 154, 156f. (128–9, 130f.)]. Alongside these citations Derrida draws up a list of the many uses of *eigen*, own, proper, and its cognates which are central to Heidegger's account of authenticity, *Eigentlichkeit*, in *Being and Time* and to his later reflections on *Ereignis*, reciprocal disclosive appropriation [*M* 159, cp. 257 (132, cp. 216)]. He hints at a link between this list and the proximity cluster *via* the etymology of the Latin *prope* and *proprius*, though he also comments that this link is lost in other languages, for example German. Whatever weight we give to this hint, can Derrida's citations of Heidegger be regarded as evidence that Heidegger's ontology is an ontology of presence? Apparently Heidegger himself explicitly proclaims that it is. However, he takes care to distinguish his fundamental ontology of presence, *Anwesenheit*, from the metaphysical ontologies which misconstrue presence in terms of what is present, *anwesend*. As in reading Derrida on Hegel and Derrida on Husserl, we are likely to find that what Derrida is getting at or, rather, towards, is more or less implicit in the Heideggerian and other texts he investigates. That this is to be expected is confirmed by Derrida's warning that we should not assume that what he calls deconstruction is denial. This warning is a repetition of the precautions issued by Heidegger. And, like Heidegger, Derrida recognises that he is in a predicament analogous to that which he discerns in the texts under analysis. It is his/our own predicament that he is deconstructing. Derridian deconstructions are auto-deconstructions, the deconstruction of Derrida and his dear reader, us.

II   WHO ARE WE?

Evidence and an ironic indication of Derrida's recognition of the delicacy of his and our predicament is the 'But who are we?' which are the last words of his essay 'The Ends of Man'. A topic of this essay is the relationship between metaphysics and humanism raised by the *Letter on Humanism* to Jean Beaufret in

which Heidegger examines the implications of Sartre's pronouncements on the relationship of humanism and existentialism. Derrida draws attention to the anthropological twist which
Heidegger's 'Dasein' is given when his translator, Henri Corbin,
followed by Sartre, render 'Dasein' as 'la réalité humaine'. If this
translation were in order it would support Husserl's complaint
that *Being and Time* is a lapse from transcendental phenomenology into anthropologism. In *Being and Time* Heidegger is no less
determined to distinguish what he does there from anthropology.
The gist of Derrida's paragraphs on this subject is that in spite
of Heidegger's disclaimer, the anthropological view of his work
taken by Husserl, Corbin and Sartre is not entirely without
foundation in Heidegger's text. For, as we have seen, although
the first part of *Being and Time* is an analytic of Dasein, there and
in his later work Heidegger's approach to Dasein is through
man. It could be said that the approach is through one man,
Martin Heidegger where it is he who is making the approach to
Dasein, and you or me where it is you or I who are making that
approach. Is not this a corollary of Heidegger's emphasis on the
concrete first person singular, *jemeinig*, nature of the point of
departure of the existential analytic?

Leaving aside this question of how we get to transcendental
phenomenology from autobiography, it is still by no means plain
how, Husserl's Prolegomena against psychologism and his pro-
liferation of reductions notwithstanding, one gets to transcendental philosophy from anthropology. This is a well-known crux.
Thus Kant proposes a critique of pure reason and a metaphysic
of morals in which transcendental arguments of one sort or
another spring from facts about man, the only instance of
rational being that we know. And in Hegel consciousness, as the
topic of phenomenology, is the truth of the soul of man regarded
as the topic of anthropology; hence phenomenology is the *Aufhebung* of anthropology and as such is knowledge which, although
it implies the end, that is, death, of man's soul as natural
phenomenon, implies at the same time its persistence, its de-
cease, as an end, as teleological *eidos* or ideal, as what we have it
in us to become. We have examined in our first two chapters the
teleologicality of Hegel's and Husserl's phenomenologies. But
any phenomenology, Derrida asserts, meaning any thinking
centred on presence or presentation – so Platonism and Heideggerian ontology are included – is necessarily a thinking of *telos* as

ideal. That Husserl's 'Idea in the Kantian sense' goes back to
Kant's idea in a Platonic sense is to be borne in mind as one
ponders the following assertion of Derrida's:

> It could be shown that at every stage of phenomenology, and
> especially whenever it is necessary to make recourse to the
> 'Idea in a Kantian sense', the powers of phenomenology are
> ruled by the infinity of the *telos*, the endlessness of the end. The
> end of man (as factual anthropological limit) is heralded in
> our thinking by the end of man (as determinate overture or
> endlessness of a *telos*). Man is what has regard (*rapport*) to-
> wards its end, in the fundamentally equivocal sense of this
> word. From all time. The transcendental end can only appear
> and display itself on condition of mortality, of a regard to-
> wards finitude as the origin of ideality. The name of man is
> always inscribed in metaphysics between these two ends. It
> has no sense except in this eschato-teleological situation. [*M*
> 147 (123)]

Here we see Derrida recapitulating what in Chapter 1 we saw
him working out in connection with Hegel's dialectic of sense
and the life and death of the sign. Anyone versed in Heidegger's
thanatology may also see here a further reason, if further reason
be needed, for including Heidegger along with Hegel within the
closure of the metaphysics of phenomenological presence. Being
towards our own death, Heidegger says in *Being and Time* and
'What is Metaphysics?', is a prerequisite of realising the possibility of being authentic, wholly present to ourselves and alive to
the sense of being.

But who are we? Derrida asks. This is a question which Hegel
and Husserl answer in transcendental terms. It is a question
which Sartre answers in the language of humanism. In the
France of May 1968 when Derrida brought his essay on 'The
Ends of Man' to an end with this question an answer in either of
these languages was no longer possible for those like Bataille and
Derrida who do not recognise Heidegger's portrait of Nietzsche
as the last of the metaphysicians but recognise instead the need
to pursue Nietzsche's programme for an 'active forgetting' of
being and of the language of metaphysics in which humanism,
transcendental phenomenology and Heidegger's own fundamental hermeneutic ontology are cast. However, as we have noted,

Derrida agrees with Heidegger that any deconstruction of metaphysics is bound to the terms of metaphysics. Indeed he at least once equates metaphysics with 'our language' [*M* 144 (121)]. We cannot therefore expect it to be easy to understand how there can be anything to say at this threshold between metaphysics and the new Nietzschean age of the active forgetting of metaphysics. But we should note that when Derrida recognises the necessity to practise an active forgetting of metaphysics, as he does, for example in his essay on 'Differance', he recognises no less the necessity to remind us actively that it is not something which can be forgotten without leaving a trace – not even in Heidegger's thinking toward a metametaphysical disclosure of being or in his own travail toward an overture which delimits the closure of metaphysics. We are confronted with an awkwardness of language like (and unlike) what Frege met in the thought that in asserting 'The grammatical predicate "is red" belongs to "this rose" ' we deprive 'is red' of the property we wish to confer upon it, namely, predicativity, and in asserting 'The concept "horse" is a concept easily attained' we convert it into an object.[2] Nor apparently in language with only ontic metaphors can this awkwardness be overcome. Where we succeed in naming or describing we describe a logocentric circle, that is to say, we are locked into the language of presence. Effacement belongs to the very structure of the trace of difference. Both concept and object become its trace, that is, the trace of a trace, the sign of a sign with no original or ultimate referent other than the 'principle' of all reference, the 'principle' of the principle of all principles, a difference older and less heeded than the ontological difference between being and beings, a difference which differs and defers itself, which is without maternal and paternal nostalgias, which is not kerygmatic, which does not dominate, which we cannot denominate [*M* 29, 76ff. (27, 66–7), *SP* 159]. In the words of Husserl which Derrida repeats, 'For all this names are lacking'.

In Heidegger's words, also words which Derrida repeats, the difficulty is that

> The difference between being and beings can subsequently be experienced as what has been forgotten, however, only if it is already discovered with the presencing of what is present and if it is thus sealed in a trace which remains preserved in the language to which being disclosively appropriates itself.

> . . . the pristine trace of the difference effaces itself once
> presencing appears as something present . . . .[3]

In Derrida's words, 'It remains that being, which is not a thing,
not a being, cannot be said, cannot say itself except *via* ontic
metaphor.'

Are all metaphors ontic, confined to the metaphysics and
language of what is presented and represented? If they are, there
would seem to be little chance of describing literally the space of
differance, since the transgression which Derrida nicknames
differance, improperly and with no sense of propriety, is, at least
metaphorically, metaphor. Only with its aid can we delimit the
transcendental phenomenological *epochē* and, more generally,
our metaphysical epoque, and pretend to explain who are the
'we' whom language keeps waiting on the threshold of metaphysics, at once profane, *mis à la porte*, because in ways we have
begun and will continue to illustrate the conceptual opposites
within our language disseminate and deconstruct themselves,
yet not *hors de portée*, not beyond metaphysics, since deconstruction is possible only in the terms of the language it deconstructs,
even if it uses (mentions? See below, Chapter 5) those terms in
inverted commas.

Near the beginning of the paper which has 'Differance' for a
title Derrida anticipates the question we have appropriated as
the title of this section from 'The Ends of Man', a paper read
later in the same year as 'Differance' was delivered:

> I take as my point of departure then, strategically, the place
> and time in which 'we' are [to be exact, the place is France
> and the time already January 1968], although my opening is
> not in the last analysis justifiable and it is always from
> differance and its 'history' as our point of departure that we
> can pretend to know who and where 'we' are and what the
> limits of an 'epoque' could be. [*M* 7 (7), *SP* 135–6]

Even if not all metaphors are ontic or ontic-ontological, our
hopes had better not be too sanguine. For the pronoun is
enclosed and opened out by inverted commas. Determination of
our epoque and putting a name to who we are and who speaks
and who dif(de)fers may be forms of mastery to which we can
only pretend.

III   A DEEP NECESSITY

Although deconstruction may turn out to be an antidote to
nostalgia for a metaphysical identity and self-containment, it is a
treatment by homoeopathy, a *pharmakon* whose remedial work is
unlikely to be complete since it employs – and, one is tempted to
say, is parasitic upon – the poison from the system it treats.

With particular reference to Heidegger's allegation that Aristotle has and is had by a 'vulgar' concept of time constructed in
terms of the metaphysics of punctively present instants, Derrida
writes in '*Ousia* and *Grammē*':

> every text of metaphysics bears within it, for example, *both* the
> so-called 'vulgar' concept of time *and* the resources that will be
> borrowed from the system of metaphysics in order to criticize
> this concept. And these resources are required the instant the
> sign 'time' – the unit of word and concept, of the signifier and
> the signified 'time' *in general*, whether or not it be limited by
> metaphysical 'vulgarity' – sets itself working in any discourse.
> It is from this formal necessity that must begin a reflection on
> the conditions of a discourse which goes beyond metaphysics,
> assuming such a discourse is possible or foreshadowed in the
> watermark of some margin or other [*s'annonce dans le filigrane de
> quelque marge* (Littré cites also the form *filigramme*)].
>   Thus, not to leave our Aristotelian moorings, *Physics* IV
> undoubtedly confirms the Heideggerian de-limitation. There
> is no doubt that Aristotle thinks of time in terms of *ousia* as
> *parousia*, the now, the point, etc. Yet an entire reading can be
> organized which would repeat in his text *both* this limitation
> *and* its contrary, and would bring out that the de-limitation is
> governed by the same concepts as the limitation. [*M* 70
> (60–1)]

Whence come the universality and necessity mentioned in this
passage? From the same place as come the universality mentioned in the passage about 'every stage of phenomenology'
which we quoted earlier and the 'deep necessity' of Derrida's
statement about Heidegger's *Anwesenheit* that 'the thinking of this
presence does nothing but metaphorize, by a deep necessity one
cannot escape by a simple decision, the language it deconstructs'
[*M* 157–8 (131)]. The 'entire reading' of Aristotle's theory of

time which Derrida outlines in '*Ousia* and *Grammē*' follows the pattern of his reading of the Hegelian treatment of time broached in the sentences on the present which we reproduced in the second section of our first chapter, and of the Husserlian treatment of the same topic which we were concerned with in Chapter 2. That Derrida has some right to claim universality and necessity can be conceded once we recognise that 'metaphysics' is a name for phenomenology understood broadly as philosophy of *phainesthai*, that is, of presentation and representation. It is therefore a teleology, for the thinking of *phainesthai* is necessarily bound to be a thinking of *telos*. This is the Platonic motif which is echoed, for example, in Kant's avowedly Platonic doctrine of Ideas and Husserl's recourse to 'Ideas in the Kantian sense'. The moment that, in Plato, for whom the architectonic archetype is the Idea of the Good, the link is made between the *eidos* as an object of possible intuition and the *eidos* as an ideal or dominant archetype which we, whoever we are, aspire to domesticate, we are at the mercy of an idea whose presence entails its non-presence to the only subject we know, ourselves. This identity and difference, defer-ence and deference, of the 'is' with respect to the 'ought to be' seems to be at any rate part of what Derrida is getting at when, especially, but not only, with Heidegger in mind, he writes:

> Isn't it this security of nearness that is being disturbed today, this belonging together and this reciprocal appropriation of the name of man and the name of being, such as dwells and dwells on itself in the language of the Occident, in its *oiko-nomia*, embedded in it, inscribed according to the gospel of metaphysics and forgotten; and also such as is awakened by the destruction of onto-theology? But this disturbance – which can come only from a certain outside – was already necessitated in the very structure which it solicits. The extremity (*marge*) of this structure was already branded (*marquée*) into its ownmost living flesh (*corps propre*). In the thinking and the language of being the end of man has been prescribed from all time, and this prescription has done nothing but modulate the equivocity of the *end*, in the play between *telos* and death. In the reading of this play one can, in every sense of the word, *entendre* the following sequence: the end of man is the end of the

thinking of being; man is the end of the thinking of being; the
end of man is the end of the thinking of being. Man is from all
time his ownmost (*propre*) end, that is to say, the end of his
belonging (*son propre*). Being is from all time its ownmost end,
that is to say, the end of its belonging. [*M* 161 (133–4)]

As regards Heidegger, it is in 'The Anaximander Fragment' that
Derrida detects hints of a 'disturbance . . . already necessitated
in the very structure which it solicits', a disturbance which
shakes the foundations of the house of being and metaphysics far
more violently than does Heidegger's transgression from ontology of present beings to ontology of the compresence of being
and man. For those who have eyes to see, the traces of this
unthinkable unheard of transgression to what is, in the words of
the title of a book by Emmanuel Levinas, otherwise than being
or beyond essence, to a past which was never a presence, a *Wesen*
which was never an *Anwesen*, are marked in the words of Heidegger's 'The Anaximander Fragment' about the difference between
being and beings which we cited in the second section. That
Heidegger fragment is recycled by Derrida with leftovers from
Hegel and Husserl to shore up differance. Differance cannot
properly be called the house that Jacques built since, for a start,
it is not built but endlessly a-building, and, secondly, it is a
house with no name, no fixed address and no construction
engineer. It is, to make use of a distinction to which we shall
return, a product of *bricolage*, improvisation, more than of engineering, and has no deeds ratified by some authoritative signature. The house of language is nomadic. It is everywhere and
nowhere since it is the un-generate pro-ducing of space: spacing,
espacement. Of it might be said, *mutatis mutandis*, what Husserl says
in a Plotinist celebration of temporality that Derrida cites and
recites:

Modifications continuously beget ever new modifications. The
primal impression is the absolute beginning of this generation
– the primal source, that from which all others are continuously generated. In itself, however, it is not generated; it does
not come into existence as that which is generated but through
spontaneous generation. It does not grow up (it has no seed):
it is primal creation.

Does this mean that a fresh now is continuously added on to the now which is modified into a not-now? Or does the now generate, spring up all of a sudden, a source? These are the images.

. . . is not the flux a succession? Does it not, therefore, have a now, an actual phase, and a continuity of pasts of which we are conscious in retentions? We can only say that this flux is something which we name in conformity with what is constituted, but it is nothing temporally 'Objective'. It is absolute subjectivity and has the absolute properties of something to be denoted metaphorically as 'flux', as a point of actuality, primal source-point, that from which springs the 'now', and so on. In the lived experience of actuality, we have the primal source-point and a continuity of moments of resonance. For all this names are lacking.[4]

Among the mediators of the differential pro-duction of language are the owls of Minerva who attempt to describe the structures of this differential production which 'belongs no doubt to the totality of an epoque, our own, but [which] has always already begun to announce itself and to *work*' [*ED* 411 (280)]. Among those, in addition to Hegel, Husserl and Heidegger, whom Derrida acknowledges to have contributed to a tracing of the structures of differance is the so-called founder of structuralist semiology.

4 Structuralist Semiology

Something is what it is only *in* its limit and *through* its limit.
Hegel, *Encyclopædia*

I POSITIONS/OPPOSITIONS

Heidegger's 'position' then is equivocal. Necessarily so, according
to what we have just found said among the comments by Derrida.
'The Anaximander Fragment' – 'Der Spruch des Anaximander',
'The Saying of Anaximander', 'La Parole d'Anaximandre' – itself
displays this equivocality. On the one hand it remains logocentric
because it posits as an end, as a *telos*, the discovery of the unique
primordial word, the *etymon*, which, without reverting to an onto-
theology of the presented, will enable us to think presencing properly.

> The relation to the pres*ent*, unfolding its order in the very essence
> of pres*encing* is unique. It is pre-eminently incomparable to any
> other relation; it belongs to the uniqueness of being itself. Thus,
> in order to name what is deployed in being, language will have to
> find a single word, the unique word. There we see how hazard-
> ous is every thinking word (*denkende Wort*) that addresses itself to
> being. What is hazarded here, however, is not something imposs-
> ible; for being speaks through every language, everywhere and
> always.[1]

On the other hand, we have just seen that in the very text from
which these lines are extracted Derrida traces traces which are
traces only of traces and signs which are only signs of signs.
Derrida draws attention to a similar equivocation in Saussure's
theorising about signs. On the one hand, Derrida points out in
Positions, Saussure calls in question the metaphysics of presence
built into the semiological theory that a sign is a representation
standing in a one-to-one relation with an abstract or concrete

43

object. This nominalist semiology, which conceives the relation of each word to its meaning on analogy with the way the name 'Fido' stands for the dog which answers to that name, is ousted by an account which subordinates whatever positivity there may be in the components of the sign to lateral relations of oppositivity, systematic negativity and diacritical difference between the components of one sign and another. It is these relations of opposition which constitute language, *langue*, the science of which would be the model for a science of signs in general, semiology, which in turn would be a part of social psychology. These relations are what are essential to language, as, employing Saussure's analogy, the rules which describe the powers of the pieces in chess are constitutive of that game. Just as the material from which these pieces are made does not matter, provided the pieces can be identified, so too the physical sounds or marks made in speaking and writing are irrelevant to the relations of which a linguistic system is comprised. Therefore, as Saussure's 'structuralist' followers have emphasised, the phoneme and the grapheme are abstractions, unheard and unseen spaces in which there is an intersection of a selection of a set of distinctive features defined in terms of such binary oppositions as vowel/consonant, voiced/unvoiced, palatal/labial, and so on. What interests the department of the science of linguistics known as phonology is the rate of systematic exchange which permits people to communicate despite variations in how they pronounce particular words. Analogously for a science of writing: 'the value of letters is purely negative and differential'. Analogously for the morphological, syntactical and semantic aspects of the sign which on Saussure's theory is a compound of an acoustic image and a concept or, as he goes on to say, of a signifier and a signified.

In spite of his critique of the nomen-nominatum model of the sign, and in spite of his dismissal of the traditional comparison of the relation of signifier to signified with the relation of body to soul, Saussure, Derrida maintains, is held by his double-deck model into the metaphysics of the 'transcendental signified'. That is, although he himself admits he would have preferred to have outlined his programme for a science of semiology without taking over from ordinary language the use of the word 'sign', his reluctant adoption of it is accompanied by an automatic endorsement of the ontology of meanings and propositions that persist unchanged though transmitted in different material envelopes which translate them from one mind to another. He remains captivated by the Cartesian dualism of body and soul, of the sensible and the intelligible.

This opposition of the sensible and the intelligible, Derrida states, is itself a manifestation of the metaphysics of the transcendental signified in so far as it carries with it the notion of a present meaning or value. The 'in so far as' (*en tant que*) of Derrida's statement admits of being taken in a stronger or weaker sense according as it does or does not imply that the opposition is sufficient to commit anyone in its grip to the doctrine of transcendental signification. In the weaker sense 'in so far as' is tantamount to 'wherever'. Derrida presumably intends us to understand his claim in the strong sense, though there is some reason to believe also that when he makes it in *Positions* its weight is borne by the premiss that where this or any of the other traditional oppositions is drawn on there is an implied reference to a self-identical subject who thinks or speaks, if only in private soliloquy. It is not quite clear that he embraces this premiss, for his words are 'the presence of something present (in the form, *for example*, of the identity of the subject, present to all its operations . . .)' [*Pos* 41 (29); my italics]. This exemplary case could also be one in which what is present and transcendentally signified is also the opposed concepts which are the objects of the subject's thoughts or utterance. The oppositions which Derrida lists are: signifier/signified, sensible/intelligible, writing/ speaking, speaking/language, diachrony/synchrony, space/time, passivity/activity. These all require some notion of subjectivity if one assumes the broadly phenomenological interpretations of time and the sign which Derrida attributes not only to Hegel, Husserl and Heidegger, but to Aristotle, Kant and the entire tradition of metaphysics. We noted in the last chapter that (as Heidegger had done, though making an exception for his own fundamental ontology) Derrida equates metaphysics with philosophy of presence which he dubs phenomenology. And Saussure is being assimilated to phenomenology of a fairly Husserlian sort. This explains why he is said to give priority to meaning. Husserlian phenomenology is as much a science of meanings as Saussurian semiology purports to be a science of linguistic and other signs. In the two alleged sciences meanings (*sens*, *Sinn* or *Bedeutung*) become 'normal' forms or, as Derrida says, values with something like the status of Platonic Ideas.

On the one hand then, if we follow Derrida's indications, Saussure is a kind of phenomenologist and a philosopher of self-consciousness. On the other hand, as Derrida also notes, he insists that 'language is not a function of the speaking subject'. And it is of course in this second fragment of Saussure's theory and the doctrine of diacritical difference of which it is a part that Derrida sees a trace of differance, spacing or tracing which one must resist classifying as either simply conscious or simply unconscious. Saussure glimpsed that something like what Derrida is alluding to, which is not just passivity or activity, *dunamis* or *energeia*, competence or performance, has to be postulated to provide an exit from the chicken-and-egg dilemma which seems to be raised by the opposition (another one from Derrida's list) of *langue* and *parole*. 'Language is necessary,' says Saussure, 'for speech to be intelligible and to produce all its effects; but the latter is necessary for language to establish itself; historically the fact of speech is always prior'.[2] A historical priority but a logical posteriority? If that is not a possible combination, could it be that both historically and logically language and speech – speech as opposed to babble – are equiprimordial? If so there would appear to be no need to postulate difference or differance to achieve an exit from the circle of language/*parole*, since the circle would not be a vicious one. However, there could still be other reasons for doing so. One of Derrida's reasons was given at the end of Chapter 1 where reference was made to his description of Hegel as the last philosopher of the book and the first thinker of writing. Differance (*et al.*) is what quite generally makes beginnings and endings possible. It became apparent in the same chapter that Derridian displacement falls somewhere between a Hegelian *Aufhebung* and a Bachelardian or Kuhnian break on the scale of continuity-discontinuity. It might also seem therefore unlikely that Derrida would hold the Big Bang theory of the origin of language for which we provided a defence a moment ago when we distinguished speech from babble. But it is unlikely that we shall find in Derrida's work any straightforward holding of theories or positing of theses in the style of traditional philosophy where sides are taken and conclusions derived or negated on the basis of ratiocinative argumentation. His disinclination for this style [*LI* 56 (225)] is not only a matter of taste. This is what causes his commentator some embarrassment when he is inclined to suggest at some point or other, as we have just done, that Derrida is guilty of *non-sequitur*. Deconstruction is no more theory than practice, an opposition he deconstructs. And deconstruction is the working through of a text to enable the text to speak for itself. Nowhere in his variations, Schubertian in their length and subtle modulation, on Rousseau's *Essay on the Origin of Languages* does Derrida enunciate a thesis on the origin of languages *in propria persona*. There as (mostly) elsewhere, his speech acts are a-thetic [*CP* 278ff., 297], speculative in a manner that dispenses with the dialectic of position and negation. So that if one does use of him the language of 'positions' or says, as was said earlier in this paragraph, that he 'postulates' something or other, these words must be used in a different, differant, dissemi-nated way [*Pos* 131ff. (95–6)]. To speak, in this way, more positively, Derrida's speech 'acts' are a *laisser faire*, where the *laisser* is neither simply passivity nor the *faire* simply activity, but something between the two which allows itself to be expressed best perhaps by the Sanskrit or Greek middle voice or perhaps by the German *lassen* which is to allow and to get done. Other-wise put, it could be said, the works of Derrida are a restless endeavour, without resting on the opposition of consciousness and the unconscious, to translate the words *il s'agit*: what is at work, what is in question . . . *was heisst Denken*? that is to say, not just what is thinking called, but what calls up thinking, tele-phonically and telegraphically.

II SYNCHRONY/DIACHRONY

In his working through of Rousseau's *Essay on the Origin of Languages* and in 'Structure, Sign and Play' Derrida refers to the catastrophe view of origins held by Rousseau and Lévi-Strauss. He remarks that although the latter says in his Introduction to the Works of Marcel Mauss that there was a switch from a stage when nothing had sense to one in which everything did, this discontinuism which suspends history in favour of synchrony does not prevent his admitting in 'Race and History' that as a matter of fact historical changes are gradual [cp., on Rousseau, *G* 283 (199–200)]. Derrida compares this with the pur(itan)ism exhibited in Husserl's tendency to ride roughshod over facts. He might also have made a comparison with Saussure's passing reference, as though it did not matter, to the fact that the cross-sections of language to be studied by semiology would be synchronic though admitting obsolescence. As the unmarried young mother said to her priest, 'But it's only a very little one'.

It seems then that with both Saussure and his structuralist follower Lévi-Strauss there is some tension between the facts of history and the theory of the synchronic interplay of oppositional difference. It is arguable that Lévi-Strauss meets this charge in the reply he gives in the chapter of *The Savage Mind* on History and Dialectic to a similar charge made by Sartre. There he tries to show that there can be a part of structuralist anthropology which illuminates the diachrony of myth. However, Derrida has a second reason for doubting whether any part of Saussure's science of language and Lévi-Strauss's science of myth can be purely synchronic. As with Hegel and Husserl, the epistemological rigour of their standard of science is both a *rigor mortis* and a hope for a *telos* hereafter of self-present presence to absolute truth. So this form of the tension in Lévi-Strauss between differential play and history leads to a tension between differential play and presence. No matter how persuasively Saussure and Lévi-Strauss may plead the pre-eminence of the lateral interplay of signifiers, no matter how ingeniously they may argue that the sense of mythemes and sememes is an epiphenomenon of non-sense, they are condemned to the philosopheme of the transcendental signified. Derrida says this not because the concept of non-sense presupposes the concept of sense, its contradictory opposite. If this were his reason it could be replied that although this conceptual interdependence holds, it does not follow that there could not *be* non-sense without sense; and anyway neither Saussure nor Lévi-Strauss denies that lots of things make sense: Lévi-Strauss's theory is precisely that in spite of the superficial inconsistency of individual myths they have an underlying non-consciously acknowledged logicality. What Derrida says does not turn on a polarity of contradictory opposites. It turns on the non-contradictory opposition of the signifier and the signified. Not only does the concept of the signifier imply the concept of the signified and vice-versa, but if there are signifiers there cannot merely be signifiers. There must also be signifieds. As with Saussure, so with Lévi-Strauss. In inheriting the sign 'sign', however cunningly he purports to deconstruct it and construct something out of it by a cannibalising *bricolage*, the transcendental signified is not transcended. He remains spellbound by a transcendental illusion.

III BRICOLAGE/ENGINEERING

Derrida diagnoses another congenital dis-ease in Lévi-Strauss's opposition of *bricolage* or improvisation and engineering.

> If *bricolage* is what we call the necessity of borrowing our concepts from the text of a more or less coherent or ruined inheritance, we ought to call every discourse by this name. As for the engineer, whom Lévi-Strauss opposes to the *bricoleur*, he would be someone who constructed the totality of his language, syntax and lexicon. The engineer in this sense is a myth: a subject that was the absolute origin of his own discourse such that its construction was 'all his own work' would be the creator of the word, the word itself. So the idea of the engineer who would have broken with all *bricolage* is a theological idea; and since Lévi-Strauss tells us elsewhere that *bricolage* is a mythopoetic, you can bet your bottom dollar that the engineer is a myth produced by the *bricoleur*. The moment we stop believing in such an engineer and in a discourse which breaks with the deliverances of history, the moment we grant that every finite discourse is bound to allow a degree of *bricolage* and that the engineer or the scientist too is a kind of *bricoleur*, the very idea of bricolage is threatened and there is a decomposition of the distinction on which its meaning depends. [*ED* 418 (285)]

Would the idea of *bricolage* be threatened, useless or impossible simply if that of the engineer were never instantiated? Does the idea of a perfect being have to be instantiated in order for the idea of an imperfect being to have instantiation and sense? It seems to me that it makes sense to say that every discourse is and must be *bricolage*; it would make sense for us to say this to someone who had the idea that some discourse was engineerage. I am sure Derrida does not endorse the doctrine of eminence and the causal theory of meaning endorsed by Descartes in the Third Meditation. I am equally sure he does not think there must be paradigm cases which furnish instances for *both* poles of a conceptual opposition; indeed, we shall soon have evidence that he thinks there need be no probative paradigm case for either pole. The Cartesian doctrines and the ontological argument from paradigm cases are fetched from the stable of transcendental signification which Derrida deconstructs. That is not enough to settle that he himself does not ride them or other horses from the same stable. As he disarmingly indicates, we and he have Hobson's choice. 'The exit "outside philosophy" is a much more difficult notion than is generally imagined by those who think they have managed it with cavalier ease, and who are usually bogged down in metaphysics by the weight of the discourse they claim to have freed from it' [*ED* 416 (284)]. This remark has a particular relevance in the context of the paper on Lévi-Strauss in which it is made, for he is one (Foucault is another) of the thinkers in France with a philosophical training who are given to protesting that they are not doing philosophy. In one sense that may be true. This leaves open the possibility that philosophy is doing them. And this is one of the things, as far as Lévi-Strauss is concerned, which Derrida's paper shows.

Lévi-Strauss imagines he is getting outside philosophy when he says, to the dismay of many of his colleagues, that his own way of working is *bricolage* and his theory of myth is itself a myth. Rather as Sartre states that dialectical thinking can only be understood by dialectical as opposed to analytical thinking, so Lévi-Strauss states that myths can be understood only by a metalinguistic theory which is mythopoetic as opposed to philosophical. Of course, he maintains that his structuralist anthropology is scientific. This theory posits deep universal unconscious structures which are the rigorous logic beneath the surface illogicality of the stories that are told. This is comparable with Chomsky's positing of universal grammatical schemata beneath the various surface grammars of natural languages. When criticised for not basing his theory on a sufficiently wide catchment of data Lévi-Strauss replies – and the comparison with Chomsky is pertinent also here – that one might as well criticise a linguist for constructing the grammar of a language before he has recorded everything that has ever been said in it. However, still like Chomsky, he allows that his theory is open to confirmation or disconfirmation by further observations. Now, like other structuralists and 'Cartesian' linguists such as Chomsky, Lévi-Strauss contends that the deep structures he posits are *a priori* and innate. It is not inconsistent to employ *a posteriori* methods to support a theory positing *a priori* structures. Derrida is not suggesting that it is. What he is suggesting is that it is naive of Lévi-Strauss to suppose that one can get away from philosophemes with saying blandly that his and all allegedly rigorous science is merely mythomorphic, empirical and empirik, that is, a pragmatic, Heath-Robinsonian making do with odds and ends. We have already explained why we do not consider such a supposition to be meaningless. But it is naive to make it without further ado. Paradoxically, 'empirical' is a philosopheme because it is used of what we contrast with philosophy. So to use it to describe discourse which is allegedly merely mythomorphic and outside philosophy is to allow that philosophy is inside that discourse: not outside, but, to give the Scots word's tail an extra twist, out*with*. Furthermore, in adopting the position that the language of his theory of myth is itself mythomorphic Lévi-Strauss is raising what Derrida calls the classic question whether any metamyth is as good as another.

IV TRUTH/METHOD

When, envisaging what he prefers to call 'a new humanism' rather than 'the death of man',[3] Lévi-Strauss proposes to treat the distinction between nature and culture as no more than methodological, it becomes necessary to put the distinction between truth and method to the test. The content of a claim to truth is not separable from the method by which it is vindicated. Truth is a result, as Hegel states the general idea expressed in the logical positivist principle that the meaning of a proposition is the method of its verification or falsification and in the different varieties of constructivist analyses of meaning and truth outlined by, for example, Wittgenstein and Dummett. (Incidentally, in the light of Derrida's deconstruction of Husserl's phenomenological intuitionism, it makes a useful connection and averts a dangerous confusion if we observe that Dummett's search for a constructivism which moderates between extreme logical intuitionism and extreme 'Platonic' realism resembles in some respects Husserl's attempt to reconcile the notion that the world is already there with the doctrine that this already thereness is constituted by consciousness, and thereby to meet the need Kant tried to meet with his doctrine of the thing-in-itself.)

A method or a strategy and a style must be sought with which to come up behind or between the oppositions of signifier and signified, the sensible and the intelligible, passivity and activity, language and speech, synchrony and diachrony, *bricolage* and engineering, myth and philosophy, philosophy and science, nature and culture, truth and method: a way of tracing the 'logic' of their complicity.

In fairness both to Derrida and to Lévi-Strauss it should be added that the former recognises places in the latter's texts where an account of such a logic could have been supplied, and that Derrida picks up the threads in those texts which serve as leads for his own efforts to supply it. There is, for instance, the place in Lévi-Strauss's Introduction to the Works of Marcel Mauss where reference is made to the blank signifiers like *mana* which in some languages, like the joker in some card games, can bear any meaning or value that may be called for to escape contradiction or anomaly, signifiers which 'mark the necessity for a *supplementary* symbolic content' [*ED* 424 (290)].

V   FROM SOUND SENSE TO GRAPHEMATICS VIA GRAMMATOLOGY

The metaphysics of presence, which Derrida equates with phenomenology, which he equates with metaphysics *tout court*, is a metaphysics of presence to self. At least since Plato thinking has been thought of as a dialogue of the soul with itself. Phenomenology is inclined to be phonological. Maine de Biran has written some paragraphs which so aptly illustrate Derrida's account of this phonological conception of understanding (*entendement*) that, although to my knowledge he does not cite them, merit citation at some length. Having noted that the eye does not light inward on itself (compare our reference in the second section of Chapter 1 to Bataille on the blind spot) and that the self-consciousness experienced in the sensations of touch depends on something outside the conscious self, Biran continues:

> But in the simultaneous exercize of hearing and voice the vocal act and the auditory modification originate in the same subject who reflects himself and rediscovers himself in the one as modifying cause or force, in the other as modified product.

. . . The sense of hearing activated by the truly intellectual exercize of speaking or the articulated voice is in fact *doubly* apperceptive or reflective; it is this sense which hears and relives everything including the most intimate modifications for which it supplies signs by which to distinguish and recall them. From this source memory borrows its own truly re-usable materials, that is to say *articulations* which address themselves to the mind's ear, come from the voice and are repeated by it at will, in contrast to simply audible sounds which come from outside and stop at the external organ whereupon a sensation is stimulated immediately.

So it is the sense proper to the understanding, that superior faculty which embraces all the others and by which the thinking and moving subject *entend*, in the full sense of the word, every idea it conceives and every action it resolves to perform.[4]

That there is a privilege accorded to hearing and the *viva voce* in the phenomenologies of Hegel and Husserl was demonstrated in Chapters 1 and 2. Although we chose not to dwell on this aspect when Derrida's treatment of Heidegger's phenomenology and later ontology was expounded in Chapter 3, we could have drawn attention there to the evidence of Heidegger's phonologism amassed in the commentaries by Derrida. The theme of nearness and approximation to authenticity which we do mention could have been developed in the terms pertaining to speaking and listening which shape Heidegger's later thinking and the phenomenological ontology of *Being and Time* where, for instance, the phenomenon of the (silent) voice of conscience is described and the hermeneutic of belonging (*zugehören*) is already being cast in the vocabulary of listening (*zuhören*).

The semiology of Saussure is also phonological. It will be recalled that his signifier is said to be an 'acoustic image'. And one of many other indications of his phonologism which Derrida reproduces from the *Course on General Linguistics* is the statement that 'The linguistic object is not defined as the combination of the written and the spoken word; this latter alone constitutes that object'. The written word is a parasitic, supplementary, secondary sign of the real sign itself whose essence and substance is the sound of the pure living voice. Writing is a merely artificial auxiliary. When, as should be done as soon as possible, we replace it by speech we have made 'a first step in the direction of truth'.

Derrida's *initial* reaction to this is to reverse the order of priority, to reassert the rights of writing. This is only an initial move because grammatology, the science of writing which promises to replace Saussure's phonological version of semiology, is discovered to be implicit in it; and semiology of a supplemented kind is discovered to be implicit in grammatology in virtue of the fact that grammatology is grammato*logy*, a *logos*, the *spoken* science of writing. In virtue of this same fact the reader of *Of Grammatology* is advised as early as the exergue of the book that a *science* under this name runs the risk of never seeing daylight [*G* 13 (4)]. Since there already seem to be sciences of writing in the ordinary sense, we must be prepared to find Derrida extending the function of the word. The adumbrated non-science of 'writing' will be graphematics. This successor to grammatology is not logocentric. It is not a logic, but a graphic.

Any study which reverses the phonologism of Hegel, Husserl, Heidegger or Saussure and simply asserts the prior or equal rights of writing is no less logocentric. This holds quite generally for all the oppositions within the logocentric tradition. It holds for Hegel's opposition of logic and phenomenology. It holds for Husserl's opposition of phenomenology to psychology, for example, for his opposing a phenomenology of internal time consciousness to Brentano's psychology of temporality. In Husserl's own teaching frequent reference to the 'parallelism' of phenomenology and psychology are interspersed with references to their interlacing.

Heidegger's distinction of beings and being, the ontological difference, is not a distinction between regional ontologies but a distinction between regional ontologies and fundamental ontology. It is a more basic distinction of level or universe of discourse than the distinctions of polar opposites which Derrida deconstructs, though he maintains that they too always have a hierarchical ordering [*M* 392 (329)]. However, Heidegger's fundamental phenomenological ontology of what conceals itself, as well as his later thinking of the meaning of being, are no less logocentric, Derrida shows, than Husserl's phenomenological ontology of what shows itself and than Hegel's doctrines of being, essence and concept. Apart from traces of something altogether other, traces which, as was shown in Chapters 1 and 2, Derrida traces in Hegel and Husserl, Heidegger's thinking, as was shown in Chapter 3, remains explicitly a thinking of the presencing of *logos*. It has now been shown that this thinking is phonological like theirs and like some of the thinking behind Saussure's semiology.

Yet, Derrida also brings out that alongside and overlapping sentences where Saussure proclaims the priority of the spoken and heard word and downgrades writing are ones which recognise, covertly or overtly, the claims of writing.

VI   THE WRITING ON THE WALL

Saussure's differential theory of the sign entails that there need be no resemblance between the sign and what it signifies. In presenting the case for these interrelated doctrines of the differential and arbitrary or unmotivated character of the sign, he draws on examples from writing. 'Since an identical state of affairs is found in this other system of signs comprised by writing we shall take it as a term of comparison to elucidate the entire question.' He then shows how communication is not prevented because a person forms a letter in an idiosyncratic way so long as there are systematic differences between the way he forms, for example, his t's, l's, and d's. This readiness to illustrate the structure of 'natural', that is, spoken, signs by appeal to their 'artificial' surrogates is the first step in the direction of acknowledging the place that must be accorded to writing if one is to plot the scope and limits of semiology. Further, Derrida points out, Saussure comes close to acknowledging the place that must be accorded writing in an extended employment of that word in which writing is not opposed to speaking, but is what enables writing and speaking in the ordinary senses of these words.

Derrida employs the ordinary word 'writing' in inverted commas or under erasure, that is, crossed out, for what he provisionally calls arche-writing.[5] This word or 'word' is provisional because although writing under erasure is in some strange way presupposed by speaking and writing in the usual meanings of these words, it does not denote an *arche* or a *telos*. It is not a *term*, whether *a quo* or *ad quem*. By ordinary standards it is a monstrosity.

The demonstration of its forms will be no easy task, for it is the
formation of form. This is why one had better not try to em-
bark immediately on graphematics, which cannot be a science,
but should pursue as far as possible the hypothesis of a science
of writing, a grammatology, prepared for the possibility that
such a science is impossible, there being no way of fixing for it a
subject matter or methodology. This is why one of his publications is entitled *De la grammatologie*, *Of Grammatology*, as
another might be entitled *De la confrontation* [*CP* 535] and as a
metaphysical meditation might be entitled 'Once more of God:
that perhaps he does not exist'. This strategy permits Derrida to
go on using the only language we know, for example, the familiar
paleonyms 'writing' and 'sign', but to graft on to these differant
and unfamiliar forces. Gradually, the risks inherent in the terms
'sign' and 'signifier', risks which Saussure and Lévi-Strauss incur,
may be diminished by substituting near-neonyms like 'mark' to
mark what occurs not only in writing but in speaking and other
kinds of mark, for example, mental images. From thinking of
signifiers standing for signifieds Derrida would wean us, *via*
speaking of signs standing for signs which stand for still other
signs, to speaking of marks which are re-marks of re-marks, and
so on. He mentions antecedents for this in the semiotic of Peirce
and the phenomenology of Lambert. Peirce defines a sign as
'Anything which determines something else (its interpretant) to
refer to an object to which [it] itself refers (its object) in the same
way, the interpretant becoming in turn a sign and so on ad
infinitum . . .'. Lambert, who, Derrida reminds us, distinguishes
his phenomenology from alethiology, the theory of truth, purports 'to reduce the theory of things to the theory of signs'.
Mention might be made too of Leibniz's doctrine that monads
are expressions of each other and of God, Berkeley's doctrine
that natural science is the interpretation of the language of God,
Locke's doctrine that most properties are signs of properties, and
phenomenalistic doctrines which have as their *telos* the analysis
of material object statements in terms of statements about
appearances, a *telos*, incidentally, which, like Peirce's definition
of the sign, is unable to dispense with an 'and so on'. However,
Leibniz's and Berkeley's doctrines are explicitly onto-theo-
logical, grounded on the principle of sufficient ground. And
Locke's properties and ideas, like the appearances of phenomenalism, are presented or presentable data. One kind of object is

allegedly replaced or represented by another. The object does not really fall away. With the mark, *alias* writing, *alias* the trace, *alias* differance, *alias* the grapheme, and so on, the object does fall away. (So too, we shall see, does the subject, without either being *denied* [*Pos* 122(88)].) Thus the 'and so on' of phenomenalism qualifies propositions which explicate propositions of a different category, for example, material object propositions. In the last analysis there is a protocol explicating statement which does not explicate another explicating statement. In principle one reaches an explicating statement which is a basic, even if open-ended, term of analysis. The 'and so on' of Peirce's semiotic, on the other hand, qualifies a series every member of which explicates a predecessor and is explicable by a successor. This is much more like what Derrida says of the mark, though he says of Peirce what he says of Saussure and Lévi-Strauss, that remarks cast in the language of signs can only be provisional. Peirce's semiotic threatens to remain a semiology, a logic of meaning and truth, on the grammatological hither side of graphematics.

VII   OF DECONSTRUCTION

On the hither side of graphematics is the first stage of deconstruction. That paleonymic stage, as is shown by the specimens of textual deconstruction we have been rehearsing in this book, consists in noting which of the terms of a binary opposition is given priority in a particular text and proceeding to reverse the hierarchic order. The risk run at this stage is that of confirming the matrix of the old regime, of preserving the ontological autonomy of sense as happens in a Hegelian *Aufhebung*. Fundamentally the old order continues. On the other hand, one may fail to see that the old order has not been fundamentally changed if one tries to make a complete and sudden break with the language of the old order, hoping to get clean outside it with neologisms [*M* 162ff. (134ff.); *Diss* 10–12 (4–6)]. So 'let us not interpret too hurriedly' [*CP* 289]. Somewhat as Saussure recognises that one cannot substitute the 'natural' spoken for the 'artificial' written word at once, Derrida recommends that we go slowly when beginning to move in the opposite direction. Only by retaining the language of the system under deconstruction can the second stage of deconstruction be reached.

Whereas at the first stage of deconstruction the oblique stroke which separates the terms of the opposition is still in place, at the second stage one *intervenes* between the terms to demonstrate that they are not terms and that the stroke is not a bar or boundary. The limit is de-limited. The stroke is stroked out; it becomes a chiasmus which marks that if one pole is parasitic on the other, the other is parasitic on the one.

The first stage of deconstruction corresponds to phenomeno-logical reduction in that it asserts: not this, but that. It is comparable in this respect with the move from thesis to antithe-sis in Hegelian dialectic, though in that dialectic the antithesis is somehow necessitated and called forth by the thesis. It is tempt-ing therefore to compare the second stage of Derridian decon-struction with Hegelian synthesis which finds a common ground for the thesis and the antithesis at a higher level. We have already established, however, that the second stage of decon-struction is a move away from meaning, truth and logic, what-ever superficial 'analogicality' (it takes two *logoi* to make an analogy) between the dialectics of Hegel and the graphematics of Derrida may be suggested by the latter's statement that 'The concept of arche-trace is in effect contradictory and disallowed in the logic of identity' [*G* 90(61)]. It is easy to mistake the force of this statement. It could be taken as an admission that in the 'logic' of graphematics the concept of arche-trace is contradic-tory. If so, the contradiction must be of a different sort from that which is accepted as unacceptable, that is, ruled inadmissible, in the logic of identity; for the latter kind of contradiction is defined in terms of truth and falsity, whereas graphematics is void of truth and falsity. On the other hand, Derrida's statement could be taken to imply that the concept of arche-trace is admissible in the 'logic' of graphematics because it is not contradictory in that 'logic'. Both of these inferences are incorrect, though perhaps to some extent excusable on account of the ambiguity of '*in* the logic of identity'. Is a self-contradictory proposition *inside* the logic constituted by a principle according to which it is ruled *out*? Anyway, the concept of arche-trace which is self-contradictory according to the principles of identity and non-contradiction, whether or not it is inside the logic which those principles constitute, is certainly not inside the 'logic' or graphic of graphe-matics. It is at best inside the logic of grammatology, though to say this is too simple, for the logical space of grammatology is the space of the threshold between the house of language, logic and being, and the nomadic homelessness of the graphematic trace. It 'is' the hyphen of the arche-trace which marks the broken-back in the anatomical structure of deconstruction itself, the *trait d'union* which is a *trait de désunion*, the hinge (*la brisure*). Deconstruction does not, as the grammarians say, construe any more than do the logocentric concepts to which it is applied. This should not surprise us. For

> In the originary temporalization and the movement of relationship with the outside, as Husserl actually describes them, non-presentation or de-presentation is as 'originary' as presentation. *That is why a thought of the trace can no more break with a transcendental phenomenology than be reduced to it.* Here as elsewhere, to pose the problem in terms of choice, to oblige or to believe oneself obliged to answer it by a *yes* or *no*, to conceive of appurtenance as an allegiance, or non-appurtenance as plain speaking, is to confuse very different levels, paths and styles. In the deconstruction of the arche, one does not make a choice. Therefore I admit the necessity of going through the concept of the arche-trace. [*G* 91 (62)]

The first stage of deconstruction is phenomenological, semiological and logocentric. The concept of the arche-trace marks the movement from the not-this-but-that of this first stage to the second stage whose both-this-and-that-and-neither-this-nor-that could be called, after Sheffer, Derrida's stroke function or chiasmus.

5　Rhetorological Semiology

Cite ... [f. F *citer* f. L *citare* frequent. of *ciēre* set moving]
Concise Oxford Dictionary

I PARACITATION

The first four chapters of this book have been occupied with an undecidability which affects what Saussure calls the signified, that is, the sense or meaning of a sign, what he earlier calls a concept. An undecidability which affects reference was explicitly touched on in the third section of Chapter 2. It is implicitly touched on however where meaning is under discussion, since understanding concepts is not separable from the ability to refer to cases instantiating them and one cannot refer to something except under some description, even if the description is no more than 'what I am referring to'. 'This is this' makes no sense.[1] Further, in the 'Platonic' theory of ideas to which are moored the phenomenological semiologies we have been considering so far, sense and reference are one.

In the present chapter we shall be less directly concerned with sense and reference than with what speech act someone is performing in uttering words which fulfil whatever the rules pertaining to sense and reference may be. And whereas in our chapters so far we have attended chiefly to the phenomenological semiologies of Continental thinkers, we turn our attention now to certain philosophers from the other side of the Channel and the Atlantic; in so doing, Derrida believes, we shall be turning our attention through 360 degrees.

In 'Signature Event Context' and 'Limited Inc a b c ... ' Derrida raises difficulties for the view adopted by John Austin in *How to do things with Words*[2] and by John Searle in *Speech Acts*[3] and his reply to *Sec*[4], that mentioning words is parasitic on using them and that the latter is therefore the normal and ordinary

60

case with which a theory of speech acts should begin, rather than with 'non-serious' cases such as the recitation of a poem or of a speech in a play, the citation of sentences in books on rhetoric, logic or grammar, and – to return to a topic aired in Chapter 2 – the employment of words in soliloquy. In these so-called non-serious cases, Austin says, and Searle agrees, speech acts suffer from 'infelicities' or 'ills' which, like those obtaining when words are uttered under duress, by accident or by mistake, are best kept apart from the infelicities to which utterances are prone in normal circumstances and to which attention must be given if the linguistic phenomenologist, as Austin calls himself, is to get off on the right foot in his task of describing the conditions under which one does this or that deed with words: make a promise, marry, congratulate, threaten, baptise a child, launch a ship, etc.;

> a performative utterance will, for example, be *in a peculiar way* hollow or void if said by an actor on the stage, or if introduced in a poem, or spoken in a soliloquy. This applies in a similar manner to any and every utterance – a sea-change in special circumstances. Language in such circumstances is in special ways – intelligibly – used not seriously, but in ways *parasitic* upon its normal use – ways which fall under the doctrine of the *etiolations* of language. All this we are *excluding* from consideration. Our performative utterances, felicitous or not, are to be understood as issued in ordinary circumstances.[5]

One of Austin's examples of infelicitous performance under ordinary circumstances is that of someone saying 'I bet' when he does not intend to pay. Although Searle seems to think so, Derrida does not deny the place of intention in the analysis of speech acts, and he allows that without it one could not make Austin's basic distinction between the locutionary act, that is, the act of saying something with a certain meaning and reference, the illocutionary act, that is, the bet, promise or assertion I make *in* saying something, and the perlocutionary act, that is, what I do *by* and as a consequence of saying something, for example, embarrassing someone, whether or not I intended to.

We have looked at some of the ways by which Derrida would persuade us that no locutionary act is meaning*ful* and that the concept of a determinate signified concept or proposition present

to the speaker's mind is a metaphysical myth. We have noted
that what he says about meaning and indication amounts to a
case also against a certain determinacy and immediacy of reference. (We could, incidentally, have mentioned in support of this
case for the indeterminacy of reference what Wittgenstein brings
to our notice when commenting on the presuppositions of pointing and naming in the course of the critique conducted in his
later work against 'the requirement that sense be determinate'
laid down in the *Tractatus*.[6]) We are therefore in a position not to
be surprised when we learn that in *Sec, LI* and elsewhere Derrida
denies determinacy, immediacy and fulness to the intention with
which a speech act is performed, even when the speaker 'fully
intends' what he says. Indeed, according to Derrida the denial of
the full presence of illocutionary (or perlocutionary) intention is
required by the denial of full presence to meaning and reference
in the locutionary act. Illocutionary intention inherits the 'writing', spacing, and re-markability of the signifier, that is, the
iterability of the type, that is, the type's exposure to the tokens
by which it is re-instantiated.

One way of iterating words is to cite them. Another is to recite
them. To Austin's and Searle's contention that citing and recit-
ing are secondary and parasitic upon serious standard uses of
words Derrida responds that the latter too are marked by
iterability. If this response is to be effective it will have to be
articulated or supplemented in such a manner as to forestall the
defence that certain ways of employing words could be parasitic
on others in virtue of a special kind of iterability which characterises the parasitic employment additional to the iterability
shared with the parasitised employment simply because they are
both cases of the employment of words; rather as genuine banknotes can be reproduced no less than counterfeit ones without
this itself entailing the falsity of the claim that there can be no
counterfeit banknotes unless there have been some specimens
of the genuine article. This comparison must not mislead us
into thinking that Derrida would not accept that the concept
of the counterfeit is dependent on the concept of the genuine.
There is no reason why he should not accept this. By the same
token he would accept the converse dependence too and the
interdependence of the concepts of the parasitic and the concept
of the parasitised. Deconstruction is not an analysis of conceptual oppositions in the abstract. When he says deconstruction is

'work' or 'labour' (*travail*) he is no doubt picking up Hegel's
reference to dialectic as the labour of the negative with a view to
deconstructing the Hegelian concept of work as a dialectic of
determinate negation; he is also adverting to the closely con-
nected notion that deconstruction is an anonymous middle-
voiced going on: *il s'agit, il se passe*, it travels, to take a simile from
Gilles Deleuze and Félix Guattari, like a rhizome.[7] But, thirdly,
in so far as deconstruction is his work, it is fitting to call it work
because it is the painstaking working through of texts where the
conceptual oppositions are operating in context, not in abstract
isolation. There could also be a displacing allusion to the displacement Freud attributes to the dreamwork.

As for iterability, Derrida tells us that this is not a concept,
hence not the genus of citationality. [*LI* 72 (244)]. It is related to
what usually goes by the name citation as Derridian writing,
tracing or differance is related to what usually goes by the name
of writing (and what usually goes by the name speaking), that is,
as what makes it possible. Put thus, it sounds as though we are
talking about a transcendental condition, but it cannot be that if
a transcendental condition is a formal concept, essence or
ground. If we can say that iterability or writing is implied or
presupposed, it is not implied or presupposed in the manner of
classical logic in which these relations hold between concepts
and propositions. Talk of factual implication or presupposition
and synthetic *a priori* conditions is liable to be no less misleading,
if what is implied or presupposed can be neither a fact nor a
proposition nor anything that could be uttered in a non-con-
stative illocutionary mode such as a regulative principle in the
philosophy of Kant or a question in the philosophies of Aristotle
and Collingwood. For all this names are lacking.

Deconstruction is therefore a sort of *bricolage*. In the deconstruction of the opposition of standard use and parasitic mention
Derrida improvises with the relatively old skin of the paleonym
'structural possibility' and pours into it (*reverser* [*CP* 163]) the
seemingly new wine of iterability. A structural possibility, unlike
a mere contingency, is at the same time a necessity, a fact, and a
value. These traditional distinctions are blurred in the 'logic' of
iterability. Should this draw the objection that 'structural possibility' is another name for necessity and that in traditional logic
too a necessity is a possibility and an actuality, it must be replied
that this classical relation leaves the distinctions between the

modalities as sharp as ever and is, in any case, a relation of entailment defined in terms of truth.

Iterability, we have noted, is a structural possibility of even 'standard', 'serious' and 'literal' talk. Why, Austin and Searle might ask, cannot the iterability in these cases be limited to the iterability within the domain of such talk? Derrida's answer is that if we are to be doing linguistic phenomenology, that is, getting back to the linguistic facts as they really are, *zu den Sachen selbst*, in Husserl's phrase, we must face the structural fact that the standard case is a serious case already riddled structurally by the canker of parasitism. It is congenitally prone to imitation, mimicry, citation, recitation. It is 'a priori' expropriated from within into the citationality of the literary and the non-literary. Its 'economy' is not restricted, but general. It could not function as a speech act unless, for example, a sentence uttered by me to you were of necessity utterable in the absence of either or both of us and when both of us are dead: every sentence is both a life sentence and a death sentence.

It will be said that Derrida is confusing what is the case with what is or must be possible. He is. Rather, he is saying that they are confused in the 'more powerful "logic" ' of graphematics. However, we may remain unconvinced by his reasons for saying this, even if we understand them. Although, as Derrida points out, Austin himself chides philosophers for making a fetish of classical distinctions like those between the true and the false and between fact and value, it cannot be assumed that Derrida's reasons for chiding them are the same. Remaining faithful, at least for the time being, to the latter distinction and to the logic in which actuality is opposed to possibility, is not the question whether on a particular occasion a promise has been made a *quæstio quid facti* and a different question from the *quæstio quid juris* which asks what conditions must be met if any promise is to be made? In *La Carte postale* Derrida elaborates a parable based on Poe's 'The Purloined Letter', the story which had been the basis for one of the seminars of Jacques Lacan. The section of Derrida's book entitled 'Le Facteur de la vérité' is a dis-semination of that seminar, but our citation of it here is made solely in order to get clearer about Derrida's response to Austin and Searle. It is sufficient to know that Poe's story concerns a letter which does not arrive at its destination. Derrida writes:

Not that the letter never arrives at its destination, but it belongs to its structure that it is always possible for it not to arrive there. [*CP* 472] . . . a letter does *not always* arrive at its destination and, since that belongs to its structure, it can be said that it never arrives there truly, that when it arrives, the fact that it is capable of not arriving afflicts it with an internal misdirection (*la tourmente d'une dérive interne*). [*CP* 517]

This particular speech act of Derrida's is a graphic constatation, a statement in the 'logic' of graphematics. It may or may not be intended to have psychological or epistemological implications. Whether this is intended or not, it is not easy to resist the thought that if the destination of the letter or the intention of a speech act is afflicted, we should be afflicted by doubt regarding any particular case. However genuine a particular case may be, it could, it seems, be fake. Any case, however standard, can in principle turn out to be deviant and derivative, not simply as a matter of empirical fact, but as a matter of logic or graphics: structurally. Classically, it is said that although at any particular moment I may be dreaming, however much it may seem that I am awake, it is idle to say that the whole of life could be a dream. It is idle, philosophers say, because if no set of conditions is allowed to suffice to justify someone's saying that he is awake, there is no cause for alarm at the assertion that we may all of us be always only dreaming, since 'only dreaming' has content only if it can be opposed to 'being awake' and if we can specify what counts as being awake as distinct from dreaming. The possibility of making this specification has been removed by the speculation that the whole of life could be a dream. Does Derrida agree that this speculation is idle? In two of the letters which comprise the section of *La Carte postale* entitled 'Envois' occur the remarks: 'I found an entire institution upon counterfeit currency in demonstrating that there is no other kind' [*CP* 192] and 'As though there were real currency, really real or really counterfeit' [*CP* 98]. God knows who the 'author' of these letters is, but if Derrida has a hand in them there might be some indication in this second phrase that he is not aiming to persuade us simply that all currency, monetary or linguistic, could be spurious or that the whole of life could indeed be a dream. What he aims to bring out is that, for example, even the statement that this or that or every specimen of this or that is pseudo, is 'afflicted', 'menaced' by an inward distraction which alienates it and exposes it to the perils of the big wide world from which philosophers in our phenomenological tradition would hope the truth of statements could be protected by the possibility of a self-contained and immediate evidence.

The upshot of this as regards Searle appears to be that Derrida has nothing against a project to catalogue the conditions prerequisite for a speech act to be a speech act of a specific kind, for example, a promise, provided it is recognised that this project posits an ideal which cannot be met by any particular speech act, since however many conditions are listed they could all be imitated by a 'non-serious' promise, including the conditions which constitute its 'seriousness'. Derrida is not denying that promises are really and truly made. He is out to show rather that we have an idealised, as Wittgenstein says, sublimed, ideal of what reality and truth consist in.

In brief, Derrida holds that Searle does not see beyond speech acts conceived as the direct expression of the speaker's intention to the indirectness of 'writing' which is inscribed into speaking. Searle asserts that although in many spheres of discourse the written word is dependent on the spoken, in logic and mathematics the order of dependence is reversed. 'The spoken, oral version of the symbols is simply an orally communicable way of representing the primary forms.' This concession, however, remains within the conceptual opposition of speaking and writing. It does not reach to the non-concept indicated by Derrida's 'writing', tracing, differance, iteration, and so on.

A similar failure to be sufficiently radical affects Searle's assertion that a theory must abtract. Derrida is surprised at Searle's and Austin's decision to base their analyses on standard examples, setting aside the so-called marginal and aberrant cases, for the latter are usually thought to be particularly illuminating for any analytic project. He is no less surprised at Searle's decision to abstract from differences of context in his discussion of the place of intention and/or intentionality in speaking and writing. Try as one may, it is not possible to do this, for 'The context is always already *in* the place and not merely *around* it' (*LI* 32 (198))]. Text and context interpenetrate. Austin, for whom the intention itself is part of the context, subscribes to this holistic principle in principle but not always in practice.

Searle asserts also that a theory of speech acts must idealise. Here again Derrida believes an explicit recognition is needed that idealisation is the invocation of an ideal *telos* or *eschaton* standing for how things should be, not how they are; yet linguistic phenomenology or linguistic analysis of the kind practised by Austin and Searle claims to be a description of ordinary linguistic conduct.

To support his assertion that the theory of speech acts must idealise Searle draws an analogy with theories in economics and astronomy. This leads Derrida to wonder what we should think of a theory of speech acts, itself a putatively 'serious' and 'literal' speech act, which has a non-literal foundation, viz. a figure of speech, an analogy. Seriously, can Searle's theory be taken seriously?

Further, an idealisation, according to Derrida, is a fiction. So do not Searle's serious theoretical statements, however literal, have a lot in common with the literary in so far as Searle is right in his view that 'most literary works are fictional'?[8] [*LI* 49(217)] At least it will no longer be possible to oppose serious and fictional discourse.

The deconstruction of this opposition will have as a consequence that the seriousness of philosophy is seen in a new light. It may be seen as compatible with the playfulness it acquires in the light of Nietzsche's answer to the question 'What then is truth?':

A shifting multitude of metaphors, metonymies, anthropomorphisms, in short an aggregate of human relations which have been poetically and rhetorically lifted, transposed, adorned, and which after long usage a certain people come to deem firm, canonic and compelling. Truths are illusions whose illusoriness we have forgotten, metaphors which have become worn and lost their sensible force (*die abgenutzt und sinnlich kraftlos geworden sind*), coins which have lost their imprint (*Bild*) and which are therefore no longer regarded as coins but as metal.[9]

Derrida compares Austin and Nietzsche in respect of their demotion of the traditional concept of truth and the contrast true/false in favour of the notion of force, in Austin's case the notion of illocutionary and perlocutionary force [*M* 382–3 (321–2)]. This comparison is made in the section of *Sec* entitled 'Parasites. Iter, of writing: that perhaps it does not exist'. The latter part of this title is parasitic on the title Descartes used in later editions for the fifth of his *Metaphysical Meditations*. The latter title is parasitic on the title used in the original edition and on the title of the third Meditation, viz. 'Of God: that He exists'. So in 'Limited Inc.' Derrida asks whether his own title can really be a title. He goes on to ask:

> On account of this parasitism, performed *in* and *by* a discourse on parasitism, is it not justifiable to regard the entire section discussing Austin as nothing more than an exercize in parody aimed at diverting the seriousness of a philosophical discourse in the direction of a literary game? Unless the seriousness of the former is already parasitized by the unseriousness of the latter, which would have serious consequences for seriousness?

These consequences would not be bound to include a revolution in the literary style of philosophy. If there is any force in what Derrida says about writing, the most serious styles of philosophy, whether penned by Hegel, Husserl, Heidegger, Austin or Searle, will be already marked by lack of seriousness. Nevertheless, it might be salutary to dramatise this somehow, for example by counterpointing analysis of what is generally perceived as a serious philosophical text with what usually passes for literature. This is what Derrida does in *Glas*. There citations of texts of Hegel and commentary are printed on the left with texts of Genet and commentary printed on the right. One of the expectations Derrida has in adopting this device is that although we are faced by what are parallel texts in geometrical space like the wings of a diptych, we shall become aware of the no-man's land of the third dimension in intertextual space.

Another expectation is that we shall become aware how simple-minded we tend to be in our decisions between what counts as citation and what as commentary. There appears to be at least a family resemblance between Derrida's deconstruction of this and other distinctions on the one hand and Wittgenstein's dissolution of problems by showing that there are commonly no necessary and sufficient conditions for something to be an instance of a concept, for example, an instance of reading, of speaking a language or playing a game, but only a family resemblance, that is, there is a property that each instance shares with at least one other instance, but no property all the instances have in common other than that of being called by the same name. Derrida considers the possibility that when Searle is challenged to say whether the words in the Cartesian title in *Sec* earlier referred to are mentioned or used he will say that they are both mentioned and used. Searle must then take up the challenge to specify where and how the line is drawn between mention and use, for that is what Searle's theory of speech acts is supposed to be able to do [*LI* 56 (226), *ECM* 33–4]. Derrida's challenge is very like the challenge Wittgenstein throws down to his earlier Tractarian self and to the practitioners of the 'Platonic-Socratic' programme of philosophical analysis which sought to locate the 'crystalline essence' of concepts. Notwithstanding this similarity between Derridian deconstruction and Wittgensteinian dissolution, it could be misleading to say that there is a family resemblance between what they do. For family resemblance as described and illustrated by Wittgenstein in paragraphs 67ff. of the *Philosophical Investigations* has to do with concepts, sense and reference seen only as topics for semiology. Although Wittgenstein breaks the mould of essentialist analysis, he does not break the mould of semiology. Derrida does, or rather he tries to show that the mould is already fissured. Hence when in the *Remarks on the Foundations of Mathematics* Wittgenstein contests the foundationalist ideals of Russell and Frege, the modifiable conventions and practices he finds where they looked for a more fixed and independent bedrock are still considered to be structures of meaning or logical grammar. For him the language games we play are still assumed to be logocentric. But it would not be difficult to supplement Wittgenstein's logocentric semiological theory with the non-logocentric, non-semiological non-theory of iterability of identity in differance and differance in identity which Derrida appeals to in order to demonstrate that foundations are already subverted. Although in exploding the solilocutary picture of meaning as a private process into meaning as a public institution Wittgenstein remains within the circuit of semiology, at least his semiology recognises a certain alterity, even if it falls short of the alterity of iteration and its Derridian iterations: writing, tracing, differance, restance, grafting (*greffe, GREPH*), and so on.

The *iter* of iterability, Derrida remarks by the way, may derive from the Sanskrit *itara*, meaning 'other', *alter*. He also remarks that if this etymology were false the shift of sense would still confirm the law of iterability asserting the corruption of the first time and place, the 'at once', the phenomenological 'moment of vision' (*Augenblick*), by the working of the other time and place [*LI* 34 (200); cp. *ECM passim*]. Compare the confirmations of this law which Derrida elicits from Husserl, and the elaborate cross-references among the manifold works to which Derrida has put what at the end of *Sec* he alludes to as his most improbable signature, a mark which indicates an area of iterability that we promised to reconnoitre in more particularity than we have so far done.

II WHO IS JACQUES DERRIDA?

Derrida's signature is improbable, that is to say unprovable or inauthenticatable, because of the iterability of indication. It is stigmatised in the manner of the first person singular pronoun whose singularly plural indexicality was discussed in Chapter 2, sections II and III. In *La Vérité en peinture* the undecidability of the 'I' is signalled by the conceit that *Ich*, the German for 'I', goes over with a bit of typographical reshuffling into *Chi*, the Greek chiasmus [*VEP* 189]. In *La Dissémination* Derrida says *Chi* is what 'it will always be possible to consider, precipitately (*hâtivement*), as the thematic design of dissemination' [*Diss* 52 (44)]. If I have understood why Derrida says *hâtivement* the implication is that it would not be quite right to think of dissemination as something that could be thematised by *Chi* or anything else, where by to thematise is meant to conceptualise. Dissemination is de-conception, diaspora of meaning and seed, hence indicable at best, if at all, by a de-sign or conceit.[10] Dissemination, differance, iteration and so on are not mastery and affirmation of a thesis, neither can they in turn be mastered logocentrically . . . or phallogocentrically, something Derrida may be hinting at when he records in connection with *Chi/Ich* that *Isch* is Hebrew for 'man' then proceeds to describe a way of pronouncing *qui* ('who') which approximates to *she*. What is only hinted at here is perhaps the Lacanian thesis which is referred to explicitly in the following sentences from *La Carte postale*:

> The affirmation of the indivisibility of the letter (which, Lacan says, cannot tolerate 'partition'), in other words of the place

and materiality of the signifier, and of the phallus as the signifier of signifiers, this affirmation of indivisibility, to describe the *faktum* of idealization, is none the less gratuitous and dogmatic even if it is required by the entire architectonic of the *Seminar on 'The Purloined Letter'* and the entire logic of the signifier. It is a philosopheme, an indemonstrable theorem or matheme . . . . [*CP* 540]

On the analysis Derrida conducts in the pages of *La Carte postale* and elsewhere the philosophemes built into Lacan's theory are discovered to be none other than those Derrida finds in the thinking of Hegel, Husserl, Heidegger, Saussure and linguistic phenomenology, above all an ideal of speech as fully adequate to itself [*CP* 498ff., *Pos* 112ff. (84ff.)]. This ideal of authenticity is incompatible with the morcelation of the 'I'.

So the author's signature too alienates as it identifies. Its 'owner' is identified as, for example, the source of the intention of identifying himself by making his mark. But his mark is a chiasmus whose expropriability Derrida marks for Derrida via a variety of near anagrams employed or suggested here and there, for example, Reb Rida [*ED* 116 (78)], Reb Dérissa [*ED* 436 (300)], De Rideau [*CP* 330] and Der-id-da [*CP* 48]. This last plays on the indeterminacy of the German *da* in respect of 'here' and 'there' and thereby exposes the fallacy of simple location one might otherwise be inclined to commit in interpreting the 'hereby' and the 'by these presents' which accompany the procedure of signing one's name. There is an allusion also to what Derrida counts as the phallusy of opposing *fort* and *da* in interpreting the now-you-see-it-now-you-don't game analysed by Freud. Derrida's iteration of the Freudian *id* will be mentioned below. As for the other concoctions, they play on the connection with Nietzsche's and Bataille's fancy that the heir to philosophy is laughter (*ris*), with Heidegger's thinking on the tear/sketch (*Riss*; cp. the torn Rembrandt at the beginning of *Glas*), and with Heidegger's notion of truth as veiling/unveiling (*rideau*, curtain; cp. the hymen, veil, sail lexicon compiled in Derrida's writings). So far, to my knowledge, Derrida has not signed himself Jack Derippa and I leave it to readers to spell out what forces might be at play in this signature if he ever did assume it. Let them not be discouraged by the 'Der'. Derrida has already observed that this approximates to the way a Frenchman pronounces 'the'. As for the double 'p', that is an iteration of 'd' licensed by Derrida's iteration of *l'antre* as *l'autre* [*Diss* 259 (229)].

The very strangeness of these typographical devices challenges the 'maintenance' some philosophers ascribe to subscription. They imagine the signature to be the expression of the kind of self-presence the token 'here-now-me' would have if one could abstract from the fact that it is the token of a type. That Searle is one of these philosophers is revealed, Derrida believes, when he says:

> Suppose you read the sentence, 'On the twentieth of September 1793 I set out on a journey from London to Oxford.' Now how do you understand this sentence? To the extent that the author said what he meant and you understand what he said you will know that the author intended to make a statement to the effect that on the twentieth of September 1793, he set out on a journey from London to Oxford . . .

'To the extent . . .' (*En tant que* . . .; see above Chapter 4, section I). There's the rub. For, says Derrida,

> at the very moment (supposing that this moment is itself full and self-identical, identifiable, for the problem of idealization and iterability arises first there in the structure of temporalization), at the very moment when someone would like to say or write 'On the twentieth . . . etc', the very thing which is to assure, beyond that moment, the functioning of the mark (it makes little difference whether it be mental or oral or graphic), namely the possibility of being repeated once more, that very thing opens up, divides and expropriates the 'ideal' plenitude or self-presence of the intention, of the meaning and *a fortiori* of the adequation between meaning and saying. Iterability alters, parasitizes and contaminates what it identifies and allows to be repeated; it brings it about that we mean (already, always, also) something other than we mean, that we say something other than what we say *and* would want to say, that we understand something other than . . . etc. In classical terms, the accident is never an accident. [*LI* 33 (200)]

Similarly where one's intention is to bear witness or to authorise by signing one's name:

the condition of possibility of these effects is simultaneously, once again, the condition of their impossibility, of the impossibility of their rigorous purity. In order to function, i.e. in order to be readable, a signature must have a form which is repeatable, iterable, imitable; it must be able to detach itself from the present and singular intention of its production. It is its sameness which, altering its identity and its singularity, divides what seals them. [*M* 391–2 (328–9)]

The accident is never an accident, according to Derrida, even where the accident is not a Freudian slip. Slips of the tongue and pen, which are psychoanalytically significant, are significant too for Derrida, allowance being made for his deconstruction of significance. That deconstruction explains that 'There is an essential *lapsus* between significations' [*ED* 107 (71)], and that no accident is an accident since there is no present substance an accident can befall. It explains why Derrida's *ipsissima verba* bristle with so many mispellings, puns and other scriptural improprieties that in citing them one feels the need to be continually adding *sic*. These *sic* jokes are serious. To adapt a remark of Geoffrey Hartman's, Derrida puns as he sneezes. This is because he cannot help thinking that this is how it is with what he calls the general text. What was said about this in Chapter 1 may now be amplified by cataloguing its liaisons with the *Es* of Lichtenberg's *Es denkt in mir*, 'It thinks in me', the 's' which Mallarmé calls the most disseminating letter, Hegel's absolute knowing, *savoir absolu*, that is, the *Sa* of *Glas*, the feminine possessive adjective *sa*, Freud's *Ça* or *Id*, Saussure's *Sa*, short for *signifiant*, the signifier, and *Sa* short for the *Speech Acts* of Sarl.

Who or what is Sarl? 'Sarl' is short for *Société à responsabilité limitée*, the more or less Limited Incorporated Anglo-American Company of John R. Searle, plus John Austin, D. Searle and H. Dreyfus, to whom Searle acknowledges indebtedness, for which it is appropriate that Derrida should appropriate the French abbreviation given that the stock of that company is not only as Continental as Hegel, Husserl, Heidegger and Saussure, but as Parisian as Ricoeur and Foucault [*LI* 11 (173)] and is probably or improbably Parisitical on Derrida *alias* Reb Rida in that he would seem to be a share- and copyright-holder in the company too, the Searles having been introduced to the Derridian corpus, Derrida says, by 'mon vieil ami H. Dreyfus'. Searle then has a limited responsibility for his Speech Acts. And so does Derrida for his. He appears to have fixed his outrageous word-plays with cunning self-wit. All his puns seem intended. But, even when one fully intends to do something, as we say, no intention is fully conscious. As Austin writes in a remark from 'Three Ways of Spilling Ink' which Derrida cites in 'Limited Ink', 'the only general rule is that the illumination [shed by intention] is always *limited*, and that in several ways'. To repeat once more, one jokes as one sneezes. One repeats as one repeats. For instance, some of the replications of *Ça*, *Sa* and so on, struck Derrida while he was writing *Glas*, others while he was writing his reply to Searle's Reply. We must beware, he would say, of saying that he had the upper hand. We must also beware of saying that the later reapplications already existed potentially in some dark pit from which they well up and make their mark as the flooding Nile might leave its watermark on a pyramid. It is not a question of deciding for activity or for passivity. The structurally iterative unconscious [*LI* 31, 45 (197, 213), *M* 389 (327)], the that, *ça*, which fissiparates intention and utterance internally and separates the one from the other by an unsaturable gap, utters and is uttered in a voice which is neither just active nor just passive, but has the force of the Sanskrit and Greek middle voice, which Latin parodies through the deponent and which French imitates when it says, for example of Searle's and Derrida's signatures, that they *s'imitent*: one can imitate them and they imitate *themselves*, as Derrida puts it [*LI* 6 (167)], though he would want to supplement this by saying that at the same time they also *s'altèrent*, s'*altèrent*.

III   METAPHOR

Invocation of the middle *voice* (of which more anon) runs the risk of a lapse into phonologism. Appeal to reflexive forms to mimic it risks the visualism suggested by the mirror metaphor of reflection [*Pas* 119]. One or the other or both of these metaphors shape(s) the understanding of understanding and sense displayed in the 'Platonists' whose texts have been cited in this book along with Derrida's recitations. Both are 'present' in the texts of Plato. They are responsible for the idea of immediate presence to consciousness which Derrida deconstructs. That idea is reinforced by the metaphor of understanding and meaning as sense, *sens*, *Sinn*, and so on. It is as though the terms for sensory perception are transferred to the intelligible perception of the eye or the ear of the mind, to the tympanum at the threshold of understanding. Hence, it should be possible, Derrida writes, spurred by Nietzsche, to take the traditional philosophical oppositions in terms of which our language is constructed and show how one of the terms appears necessarily as the differance of the other, as the other differed in the economy of the same, for example, the intelligible as differance of the sensible, as the sensible differed/deferred, the concept as differance of intuition, as intuition differed/deferred, etc. [*M* 18 (17), *SP* 148–9].

In addition to these hints in the direction of a diaphoristic (another topic of which more will be said in Chapter 6), one finds in Nietzsche at the same time the metaphor of concepts as coins which have lost their visible and tangible imprint through repeated use. In Hegel too one finds the statement that 'the first sense is sensible, the second spiritual', this latter being a result of the effacement through usage of the metaphorical force borne by the former [*M* 268 (225)]. As conceived by Hegel, Derrida observes, this process is none other than the semiological *Aufhebung* described in the first section of our first chapter. In 'White Mythology', *Of Grammatology*, *L'Archéologie du frivole* and elsewhere Derrida refers to a number of other writers, among them Rousseau and Condillac, who consider that language is originally metaphorical and who described the dying of metaphors in terms of the metaphor of wear.

Since wearing down is a continuous process, it is not likely, in view of what was said in the last section of our first chapter, that Derrida would consider that this metaphor could tell us the first and last word about language. On the other hand, it appears from all our chapters that there is a reliance on metaphors in Derrida's own discourse, supposing they can be distinguished from the metaphors in the texts (of) which he treats. The present chapter has noted what he makes of Searle's appeal to analogy in support of his theory of theory. One could be forgiven for concluding therefore that Derrida himself endorses the idea that language, hence philosophy, is fundamentally metaphorical. Would this not be a corollary of his deconstruction of the oppositions of the literal and the literary, the literal and the fictional, the literal and the figurative? Does it not follow from that that the literal *is* figurative?

What is Derrida's philosophy of metaphor? What, in particular, is his philosophy of the place of metaphor in philosophy?

What is a metaphor? By now we have learned not to expect from Derrida, any more than from Wittgenstein, an answer to such questions which catalogues sufficient and necessary conditions. We have learned not to expect an answer. His projects are prosecuted through the contexts of what other writers have written. The writings of Jacques Derrida are parasitic. So, when it is the Aristotelian text for example which is being explored he is willing to wait and see whither we are taken by the idea that metaphor is a genus of which the species are analogy and any other tropes where the motivating force is resemblance of some sort. Now resemblance is the motivating force whenever a categorematic word is re-used, for example when the word 'man' is used for Socrates, then of Plato or of Socrates again. If calling Socrates a man for the second time is metaphorical, so too would be the description of something as such-and-such in virtue of a family resemblance, and so on up the scale of increasing difference, however that is measured, until we reach what in the abundant literature on metaphor is commonly referred to as a metaphor which is 'truly creative', itself a description which admits of degrees. As to the minimal, thin end of this scale, few of those who have written on the subject, including Aristotle himself most of the time, would say that a word was being used metaphorically where the only duality was that of the tokens (e.g. 'man' and 'man') or the referents (e.g. Socrates and Plato, or Socrates today and Socrates tomorrow). They would require a duality of meaning, usually a duality of ordinary or standard or normal or proper meaning and meaning which is not so regarded. This requirement would entail that applications of a term in virtue of an institutionalised family resemblance would not be metaphorical. Consider Dugald Stewart's account of family resemblance, what he called, following Payne Knight, the transitive or derivative applications of words:

Suppose that the letters A, B, C, D, E, denote a series of objects; that A possesses some one quality in common with B; B a quality in common with C; C a quality in common with D;

D a quality in common with E; while at the same time no quality can be found which belongs in common to any *three* objects in the series. Is it not conceivable that the affinity between A and B may produce a transference of the name of the first to the second; and that, in consequence of the other affinities which connect the remaining objects together, the same name may pass in succession from B to C, from C to D, and from D to E? In this manner a common appellation will arise between A and E, although the two objects may, in their nature and properties, be so widely distant from each other, that no stretch of imagination can conceive how the thoughts were led from the former to the latter. The transitions, nevertheless, may all have been so easy and gradual, that, were they successfully detected by the fortunate ingenuity of a theorist, we should instantly recognise, not only the verisimilitude, but the truth of the conjecture; in the same way as we admit, with the confidence of intuitive conviction, the certainty of the well-known etymological process which connects the Latin preposition *e* or *ex* with the English substantive *stranger*, the moment that the intermediate links of the chain are submitted to our examination [*e, ex, extra, extraneus, étranger, stranger*].[11]

Someone's use of a word is metaphorical, most rhetoricians would agree, only where the 'affinity' of which Stewart speaks has not been recognised as part of what the word itself means. The application must still be 'transitive' or extended, and there must be a non-transitive, literal way of describing the referent.

Now the 'metaphors' which Derrida introduces in his deconstructions are indeed extended uses of words, and this extendedness is sometimes signalled by their being printed in inverted commas or under erasure or by their being improperly spelled. However, they are extended uses of words for which there exist no words for describing the same thing which are taken to be non-extended and literal. For example, there is the writing which occupies a measurable space on this page, and the Derridian 'writing' whose 'space' has no name; and there is the difference which is opposed to identity in classical logic and the différance which is a mongrel neographism. Derrida uses the second items in these pairs not metaphorically, if a metaphor requires the two conditions mentioned in the preceding paragraph. He uses them catachretically, where 'catachresis, in general, consists in a sign which is already attached to a first idea being attached also to a new idea which had no or no other proper sign in the language', allowance, *Spielraum*, being granted for at least the second occurrence of 'idea' in this definition from Pierre Fontanier.[12] Indeed the catena of catachreses is being continually extended by Derrida to reduce the danger of their being mistaken for metaphors as his neographisms become so familiar through our bandying them about that it is easy to think we understand their sense. We do not. There is no sense to be understood.

Derrida's location of these catachreses on the threshold of sense, the blank *marge de sens* [*Diss* 283 (251)], distinguishes them from the Platonic catachresis *eidos*, idea. Derrida calls *eidos* a metaphor, meaning that in the Platonic theory of ideas the meaning of *eidos* is extended from the context in which it is a sensible image seen in the natural light of the sun. If the word 'metaphor' is employed so broadly, as Aristotle employs it, for any transferred use of a word, including catachresis, the fundamental words of philosophy which Heidegger calls *etyma*, for example, *eidos, logos, theoria, aletheia* and so on are all being used metaphorically; as too are the fundamental words of rhetoric, for example 'metaphor' and 'catachresis'. Any metaphorology or philosophy of metaphor therefore begs its own question. It assumes as understood the theme it aims to describe. It cannot command a survey of its subject-matter. It has a blind spot, like Bataille's eye. There can be no coherent philosophy of the place of metaphor in philosophy.

In particular, since the metaphorical use of a word is a transference from a literal proper sense of a word, and since, as this book has tried to demonstrate, Derrida deconstructs literality and propriety, Derrida thereby deconstructs the metaphorical. *Plus de métaphore*, as French ambiguously puts it. Either everything we say is metaphorical, that is, we move from one metaphor to another interminably; or nothing is metaphorical; or neither and both.

Lest the import of what has just been said be misunderstood, let it be added that what is at stake is a philosophical theory of metaphor and the part metaphor plays in the philosophies of, say, Plato, Leibniz, Bergson or Derrida. Derrida is not denying that one may be speaking the literal truth when one says such things as 'This pencil is red', any more than he is denying that there are objects we refer to and persons who refer to them. It is a certain construal of sense and reference that he deconstructs, namely, that which seeks to secure itself to the idea of theory as direct seeing, to the theory of the *eidos* as an immediate presence to mental vision, and to the thought of *logos* as hearing oneself speak. These are the philosophemes whose trail Derrida pursues through the 'Platonist' texts of dialectical semiology, transcendental phenomenological semiology, fundamental ontological semiology, structuralist semiology and rhetorological semiology.

He pursues it too through the *Phædrus* and through other texts of Plato. Ironically, in more than one of these, as in the texts of Hegel, Husserl, Heidegger, Saussure and so on, the trail leads to the general text and its thresholds of dissemination. Perhaps the Good Father, the Sun and the Absolute Ghost do not after all command a logocentric survey. Perhaps the sovereignty of Good according to Plato is the sovereignty according to Bataille. Maybe Plato's catachresis has to go through catacrisis. The oracle may be estranged from itself. The decision to commit parricide may have to be made.

> STRANGER: We shall find it necessary in self-defence to put to the question that pronouncement of father Parmenides, and establish by main force that what is not, in some respect has being, and conversely that what is, in a way is not.
> THEÆTETUS: It is plain that the course of the argument requires us to maintain that at all costs.
> STRANGER: Plain enough for the blind to see, as they say. Unless these propositions are either refuted or accepted, anyone who talks of false statements or false judgement as being images or likenesses or copies or semblances, or of any of the arts concerned with such things, can hardly escape becoming a laughing-stock by being forced to contradict himself.
> THEÆTETUS: Quite true.
> STRANGER: That is why we must now dare to lay unfilial hands on that pronouncement . . . .[13]

What the Stranger prefers to see as the severing of the filial tie rather than as the severing of the father's head opens up the *Spielraum* in Plato's text where differance and writing come into play. Already in the *Phædrus*, where Plato's phonologism is most conspicuous, natural inner writing that speaks is a metaphor of the true word and living memory, *mneme*, in contrast to artificial,

external, dumb writing which is Plato's metaphor of dead language and the aide-mémoire *hypomnesis* [*Diss* 172 (149)]. But in
the *Republic*, *Sophist* and *Philebus* occur passages which point
beyond being and 'beyond all the oppositions of "Platonism"
towards the *aporia* of originary inscription' [*Diss* 185 (160)],
towards 'a certain invisible and formless medium which receives
everything and participates in the intelligible in a very curious
manner which is difficult to understand'. After citing this and
other statements about the receptacle, *chôra*, from *Timæus* 48–51,
Derrida cites the passage from *Timæus* 52 referring to what is
neither sensible nor intelligible and can be treated of only by a
cross-bred kind of reasoning: pre-logical space, or spacing, as
Derrida would put it, to mark the temporal, diachronic aspect of
the spatio-temporal *espacement* of the 'originary' writing which
makes possible and impossible the purely synchronic or achronic
logical space of which Wittgenstein speaks in the *Tractatus*.

It is to metaphors from writing and grammar that Plato has
recourse when he attempts to describe the topic of this mongrel
reflection, the mute, blank *topos* which must supplement the *eidos*
if there is to be any dialectical interweaving of the ideas.

> This writing (is) *epekeina tes ousias* [beyond beingness or pres-
> ence]. The disappearance of truth as presence, the vanishing
> of the present origin of presence, is the condition of all (mani-
> festation of) truth. Non-truth is truth. Non-presence is pres-
> ence. Différance, disappearance of originary presence, is *at the
> same time* the condition of the possibility and the condition of
> the impossibility of truth. At the same time. 'At the same time'
> means that being present (*on*) in its truth, in the presence of its
> identity and the identity of its presence, *doubles itself* the
> moment it appears, the moment it presents itself. *It appears, in
> its essence, as* the possibility of its own duplication, that is to say, in
> Platonic terms, of its ownmost non-truth, of its pseudo-truth
> reflected in the icon, the phantasm or the simulacrum. It is not
> what it is, identical and identical with itself, unique, except in
> *adding to itself* the possibility of being *repeated* as such. And its
> identity is made hollow by this addition, vanishes in the
> supplement which presents it. [*Diss* 194 (168)]

There is therefore no repetition of the intelligible, self-identical
eidos and the type without repetition of the sensible phenomena

and tokens. If we can see this as a viable reading of Plato, we can see why Derrida says, apocalyptically, that we are on the eve of Platonism [*Diss* 122–3 (107)]. He also says that it would be natural to think this the morrow of Hegelianism. Bearing in mind what was said in our first chapter, we cannot suppose Derrida to be denying that this morrow is an aftermath. He immediately warns us once more against thinking in terms of the overthrow of *philosophia* and *episteme*. When we say that the two kinds of repetition, the repetition of life and the repetition of death, are related according to the logic or graphic of supplementarity, we are saying that

> we can no more 'separate' the one from the other, think one without thinking the other, 'label' them, than in *the pharmacy* we can distinguish the remedy from the poison, the good from the bad, the true from the false, the inside from the outside, the vital from the mortal, the first from the second, etc. Thought within this original reversibility, the *pharmakon* is the *same* precisely because it has no identity. And the same (is) in supplement. Or in differance. In writing. [*Diss* 195 (169)]

The 'we' here includes Derrida. He is not *au-dessus de la mêlée*, as we have insisted throughout this exposition of some of his writing. As we must insist now, he is not doubting that we ordinarily doubt only where there is a concrete reason for doing so here and now. Is the 'structural possibility' of repetition therefore a merely philosophical hyperbole, not a real reason for real doubt? It is the condition of the possibility of doubt. It is also what makes not doubting possible, and impossible. Ordinary language and the philosophical: where is the line of demarcation? The so-called ordinary language philosopher may think that Derrida's susceptibility to irritation by the structural possibility of iteration, his sensitiveness to the 'threat' of a speech act's failing to reach its destination and to the non-presence which 'torments' the here and now arise from his being haunted by too Husserlian, too Hegelian, too Cartesian, too 'Platonic' an ideal of presence and presence to mind. In one of the missives collected in *La Carte postale* occur the words:

> Me, I am a man of my word (*un homme de parole*). I have never had anything to write. When I have something to say I say it

or say it to myself. Basta. You are the only one to understand why I have found it absolutely necessary to write precisely the opposite, on the question of axiomatics, of what I want, of what I know I want, in other words of you: the living word, presence itself, proximity, proper sense . . . . [*CP* 209]

And in a later letter:

You have always been 'my' metaphysics, the metaphysics of my life, the 'verso' of everything I write (my desire, the word, presence, proximity, law . . .). [*CP* 212]

Could Derrida 'himself' have truly intended what these self-addressed words say? It is not clear, any more than it is clear which side is the recto and which the verso of a piece of paper or a picture postcard. It is clear that for anyone who is ever inclined to repeat these words (and which of us is not?) the writings of Derrida will be a *pharmakon*. This inclination is manifest in the desire to 'place' him and his writings in the context of the History of Western Thought, a desire that has been indulged so far in the chapters of this book, will motivate the chapter to come, and will doubtless survive its re-capitulation.

6 Anasemiology

Rien n'aura eu lieu que le lieu

Stéphane Mallarmé

I THE GENDER OF TRUTH

Pharmakon is one of those syllepses in whose undecidability Derrida takes no less delight than Mallarmé takes in the resonances of *hymen*[1] and than Hegel takes in the oxymoronic semantics of speculative words like *Aufhebung*.[2] But it is not simply the words that interest them or the word play to which they give rise [*Diss* 249 (220)]. What interests them primarily is rather that from which such words arise, that of which they are symptomatic. Derrida's response to this question is different from Hegel's. This difference, it might be said, grossly oversimplifying, is due to the fact that between Hegel and Derrida comes Mallarmé; and Nietzsche. In the present chapter an attempt will be made to substantiate this statement while bringing out why it is a gross oversimplification. This will call for an amplification of the brief references made to the middle voice in the preceding chapter and a resumption (in Chapter 7) of the task begun there of showing what relevance, if any, Derrida's work has to the preoccupations of such post-Fregean philosophers as Wittgenstein, Quine and Goodman, Proprietary Ltd.

Speculative thought in Hegel's sense is the two-faced thinking of reason as opposed to the dogmatic one-sided thought of understanding which conforms slavishly to the principle of non-contradiction. This one-sidedness is not overcome when it is asserted, for example, that the absolute is the unity of the subjective and the objective. This assertion is in order as far as it goes. But it goes no further than Schelling is willing to go in limiting *Aufhebung* to the construction of an identity of opposites. This falls short of truly speculative *Aufhebung* in which both the identity

83

and the difference of opposites is recognised.[3] This recognition is
embodied in Hegel's doctrine of absolute difference described
above in Chapter 1. So could it be said that Hegel expounds a
philosophy of deconstruction in response to Schelling's philosophy of construction? That we should not merely be bandying
words in thus tightening the threads between Hegel and Derrida
is indicated by Hegel's comment on the double use of *aufheben*,
for both annul and preserve, that it illustrates 'the speculative
spirit of our language rising above the mere "either-or" of
understanding.'[4] Does this not anticipate the second stage of
deconstruction which, after the first stage has affirmed this and
denied that, proceeds to affirm both this and that? And does not
Koyré's comment with reference to this both-and force of Hegel's
speculative words, that Hegel 'makes no choice', mirror Derrida's statement that in the deconstruction of the *logos* one does not
make a choice?[5] Mirroring there is, but a mirror can distort, as it
does here if it leaves us with the impression that the chief
difference between Hegel and Derrida can be expressed in the
formula that whereas Hegel affirms the identity of identity and
difference, Derrida affirms their difference. Since Heidegger distinguished the ontic formal concept of identity from the same,
belonging together, *Ereignis*, which is the ontological condition of
conceptual identity and difference, there can be no simple reversal of Hegel. It was not a reversal we were witnessing when in
our first chapter we saw Derrida questioning Hegel's doctrine of
an ultimate identification of knowing and the known, a doctrine
which leads him to see in Hegel's dialectic 'the most ample and
impermeable umbrella against undecidability.'[6] Nor was it this
which we witnessed when in Chapters 2 and 4 we followed his
pursuit of phonologism in the pages of Husserl and Saussure, or
when in Chapter 3 we watched him levering wide the crack he
had detected in the very condition of identity and difference to
reveal evidence of differance, if not the *Sache selbst*: an ana-
ontological residue the 'presence' of which, as Derrida also
revealed, had come to be suspected by Heidegger himself. But it
is from Nietzsche and Mallarmé that Derrida learns the styles in
which to treat of this residue, of, in the words of the subtitle of
Glas, what is left over of and by absolute knowledge.

Nietzsche sees in philosophy, as Hegel soon saw in the philosophy of Schelling, indifference to difference, a neutering of becoming, 'adiaphoristic repression'. If becoming is to be given its

due, if the heir of philosophy is to be the heir of Heraclitus and recognise that differance, which is not the identical, is yet differance *of* the same, what is called for is a strategy which is diaphoristic without being negatively dialectical. This strategy will

> take up again all the coupled opposites on which philosophy is constructed and from which our language lives, not in order to see opposition vanish, but to see the emergence of a necessity such that one of the terms appears as the differance of the other, as the other differed within the economy of the same (the intelligible as differant from the sensible, as the sensible differed; the concept as intuition differed-differant; culture as nature differed-differant; everything that is other than *phusis* – *technē, nomos, thesis*, society, freedom, history, spirit – as *phusis* differing: *phusis in differance*). [*M* 18 (17)]

Differing-deferring is active and affirmative interpretation which, without being a hermeneutic quest for some central nucleic truth, at the same time 'determines the noncentre otherwise than as loss of centre' [*ED* 427 (292)]. It is not the negation of the hermeneutic enterprise. Today, at least, there is no question of choice. There is no call for the either-or. The either-or belongs to the grammar of traditional metaphysics. As Nietzsche observes, 'The fundamental faith of the metaphysicians is the faith in antithetical values.'[7] So we subscribe to that faith when we deny it. As Derrida says in *Spurs: Nietzsche's Styles*, 'It is here that in its turn the opposition between metaphysics and non-metaphysics reaches its limit, which is the limit even *of* the opposition, of the form of opposition. If the form of opposition, the oppositional structure, is metaphysical, the relation of metaphysics to its other can no longer be that of opposition' [*Spurs* 116f.]. This only appears to conflict with Derrida's assertion in the passage quoted from 'La Différance' that opposition does not vanish in diaphorisation. There he is thinking of the Hegelian dialectic in which opposition is negative and where, although opposition vanishes in the course of the dialectic, it is still a negative opposition, the negation of negation, which leads to this appropriation in a higher position. Now it would be careless to infer that because diaphoristic interpretation is said to be affirmative it therefore must go in for position, thesis. Nietzschean transvaluation of values is neither thetic nor antithetic in the style of

negative dialectic. It effects not a change in values but, as Gilles
Deleuze puts it, a change in the element from which value derives
its value.[8] According to Heidegger, however, when Nietzsche says
that in abolishing the true Platonic world we abolish also the
apparent, his alleged reversal of metaphysics condemns him to
remain a prisoner of metaphysics. Derrida agrees with Heidegger:
'the Nietzschean demolition remains dogmatic, as do all reversals,
imprisoned in the metaphysical edifice that it sets out to destroy' [*G*
33 (19)]. But Derrida also agrees with Deleuze. Once again we
discover that Derrida is a double (*deux*) reader. (We have already
begun to discover that Derrida is also a de-reader, a double reader
of the 'of' of property, possession and genitivity or, more properly,
de-generation.) There is a lot to be said for Heidegger's reading of
Nietzsche. 'Heidegger, however, does not restrict himself (as it is
often supposed) to this schema of inversion. Still, he doesn't purely
and simply abandon it, for the work of reading and writing is no
more homogeneous in this case than it is in Nietzsche's, and his
seeming leaps from *pro* to *contra* are not without a certain strategy'
[*Spurs* 79]. How can we account for the heterogeneity of Heidegger's reading? How can he both agree with Nietzsche that transvaluation must transform the hierarchical schema itself, and at the
same time abide by a classically hermeneutic search for truth
which such a transvaluation would render anachronistic?

The source of this self-deception or a further symptom of it,
Derrida suggests, is the way Heidegger responds, or fails to
respond, to Nietzsche's remark about the Platonic idea of truth
that 'It becomes woman', *sie wird Weib*. Derrida points out that
although Heidegger cites this phrase, there is no discussion of it
either in the two volumes of his *Nietzsche* or apparently elsewhere. Derrida's discussion offers clues to a reading of Nietzsche
and of Heidegger's Nietzsche which moves at a tangent from
metaphysics, from fundamental ontology, and from the hermeneutic circle of the question of the meaning of being. On this
reading, the Idea in its first form is the truth attainable by the
wise man: 'I, Plato, am the truth.' Truth is phallogocentric and
anti-feminist. Woman is error. When truth becomes woman it
becomes unattainable, Kantian – categorically imperative – and
Christian – consoling, castrated and castrating. Transcendental,
beyond the philosopher's reach, enigmatic and seductive, this
feminine truth gives herself out as castrated by herself and at the
same time castrates and masters the master at a distance. At this

stage she is both truth and untruth. But because this negative, reactive truth is the negation of phallogocentric truth, it belongs to the restricted economy of phallogocentric truth. At the third stage of this genealogy of truth this double negation is transcended and feminine truth affirms itself as a dionysiac play of artful perspectives in the knowledge that if truth is unknowable it is not consoling or binding, and that 'with the true world we have also abolished the apparent.' There was no thing (in itself) to castrate, so no loss to lament; 'it had never been'; 'la castration n'a pas lieu.' However, if the position arrived at in this third stage is to be a conclusion or a synthesis derived from the first two stages according to the logic of Hegelian dialectic or some other hermeneutic scheme, it must be possible to decide what counts as truth, as woman, as castration, and what counts as their opposites. Indeed this must be possible if one is to plot the relations of these stages in an order which is genea*logical*. But all logical codification, all genealogical direction, all systematic semiology, in a word, sense, is subverted if, on the one hand, there is logic and sense only where there is determinacy, that is, where of a pair of opposites the affirmation of one implies the denial of the other, and if, on the other hand, undecidability is all-pervasive; as it will be if the stroke that marks the threshold between the opposites is a connective and disconnective of the logic of the supplement, *pharmakon* or hymen: a logical inconstant, as it were.

This graphic is displayed by *pharmakon*, because *pharmakon* is not just poison nor just cure [*Pos* 58–9 (43)] yet both poison and also cure, and it straddles the two attitudes to writing of which Socrates treats in the *Phædrus* and which Derrida treats in 'La Pharmacie de Platon'. There, using language similar to that of the comment which Deleuze makes about Nietzsche's transvaluation of values, Derrida writes of the *pharmakon*, arch archewriting, that it is 'ambivalent' so that it can constitute the milieu (*milieu*) in which opposites are opposed [*Diss* 145 (127)], as a milieu is 'itself' both centre and circumference, text and context. And in 'La Double séance' he cites Mallarmé's description of the hymen, which is both consummation and the barrier that prevents it, as *milieu, pur, de fiction* [*Diss* 242, 244 (214, 215)]. In both essays and in *Spurs* he warns against the trap of supposing that the graphic in question is a third value. The medium in question is no static coincidence of opposites (Nicholas of Cusa). And its undecidability is not that of an included middle like the neither-provable-nor-disprovable of Gödel's proposition. The lieu of the milieu is not a position or a proposition. It is instead in stead, in lieu, of a position, at most a pro-position, an *Ersatz*. If Nietzsche had propounded and proved undecidability like some Gödelian God, he would have given the game away. The game must be a double game, a game that one plays with two hands. As Derrida noted in another reference he makes to Gödel as early as his Introduction to Husserl's *Origin of Geometry*, 'undecidability has a revolutionary and disconcerting sense, it is *itself* only if it remains essentially and intrinsically haunted in its sense of origin by the *telos* of decidability – whose disruption it marks' [*O* 40 (53)]. This entails not only that the propounding of undecidability is a move in the logocentric language game of truth. It means that even the mere entertainment of the idea of undecidability forestalls a clean break from the logocentric circle. And with this both Nietzsche and Derrida would agree. In that case, why don't they take the view that one might as well be hanged for a sheep as a lamb? Why, if we are condemned to logocentrism willy nilly, don't they embrace logocentrism willy? Nietzsche doesn't because, very roughly speaking, he is in favour of health and he sees this to be impeded by the idea of categorically obligating truth. Derrida doesn't because he is struck by the way that when one follows out actual texts employing certain classical oppositions to their logical conclusions one discovers that these conclusions are not entirely logical. Not not logical because they simply contravene the principle of identity, but because the prior logic of supplementation prevents one finding identities to which that principle would apply. There is just innocent becoming, heteroclitic, Heraclitean flux with regard to which the only posture that is not unbecoming is a 'naivety withdrawing into an unconscious, the vertigo of non-mastery, a loss of consciousness', and the only style the plural style of parody. Poietic, sung (whistled?) parody, not calculated parody in the service of prosaic truth, for that would be to fetch down once more the tablets of the law [*Spurs* 101]. This is the voice in which Nietzsche announces the three perspectives on truth, the interpretations which are *his* interpretations, and at the same time not his, but spoken in a middle voice, as if, as with Derrida, his words were flanked by invisible quotation marks, making a mock of our attempt to fix his position.

Derrida has investigated this predicament, ours and his, in further comments provoked by Nietzsche made subsequent to *Spurs* at Montreal, Edinburgh and elsewhere. In responding to a participant in the colloquium at Montreal he admits to being taken aback at the way in which, in North America and France at least, the deconstruction industry boomed, particularly among those who saw in it an implied reference to structuralism. For him 'deconstruction' had been but one handy tool among many in the range which included also differance, writing, tracing, spacing, restance, pharmakon, hymen, supplement, and so on. He never saw in deconstruction the negative force with which others endowed it and which, to his embarrassment, he now finds himself expected to endorse. 'I believe in the necessity also for a dismantling of systems, I believe in the necessity for an analysis of structures in order to see how they function, whether successfully or unsuccessfully, or why the structure fails to lock into itself, etc.. But for me this was far from being either the first or the last word, and in particular it was not intended to be a password for everything that was to follow' [*OA* 117–18]. But the fact that Derrida says he does not subscribe to this programme according to which deconstruction is a technique that merely takes systems apart should not be allowed to conceal the fact that he relates this piece of intellectual autobiography to illustrate the paradox of the addressees (*paradoxe des destinataires*) and its corollary, the paradox of the signature. An author's intellectual autobiography is an otobiography. There is no simple distinction between what someone says and how he is heard, so 'Plato's signature is not yet complete'. The paradox of the signature or the proper name is that 'it is always the same thing but it is each time different' [*OA* 116]. Otherwise expressed, 'plus c'est la même chose, plus ça diffère'. Derrida's gloss on this has what may seem a surprisingly Lévi-Straussian or Chomskian ring. Speaking of Augustine, Montaigne, Rousseau and Nietzsche, thinkers for whom philosophy has been inextricably autobiographical, he appears to allow that autobiographies may be singular idiosyncratic substitution instances of the same achronic law, the filling of an *a priori* schema. But it is not really surprising that he should say this in the context of a discussion in which he is wishing to make it plain that with him deconstruction had not been conceived as a weapon of war to be used *against* philosophical structures, not even against the structures of structuralism.

Faintheartedly, I reported Derrida's paradox of the addressees as the paradox that the signatory's intellectual autobiography is not a simple contrary of how he is heard. My 'intellectual', however, sugars the Derridian pill. He queries the standard distinctions between the exoteric and the esoteric, between a writer's doctrine, which is public property, and his private life which, so it is said, is not. Is Husserl's anguish over the crisis in European science part of his private life or is it part of an impartable philosophical doctrine? And whatever one may say of, say, Kierkegaard, it can hardly be said of Husserl that he is tender-minded, much less that he is soft in the head.

II   THE MIDDLE VOICE

The *paradoxe des destinataires* (and the addressees may include the sender, the *expéditeur*) is the paradox of the generality of text. We can hope to get a firmer grip on it and at the same time on what Derrida means by *milieu* if we now consider how we should understand his references to the middle voice. Let us ask first what has been said on this subject recently by two theoreticians in the field of linguistics.

Jan Gonda and Emile Benveniste agree in rejecting a traditional view that the middle voice indicates an interest that the subject has in the action. For could not the subject have an interest in the action when this is indicated in the active voice? I do not accept this traditional view as stated because it is too vague. It does not distinguish, for example, someone's taking an interest in something from someone's having an interest in something, that is, being affected by it, whether or not he is aware of the fact.

Benveniste contrasts the active and the middle voices as follows:

> In the active verbs denote a process which is accomplished from (*à partir de*) the subject and outside him. In the middle . . . the verb indicates a process of which the subject is the seat (*siège*); the subject is interior to the process.[9]

This is puzzling. If the subject is the seat of the process, how can he be interior to it? Is it not rather interior to him? No wonder Gonda finds Benveniste's account unclear. It becomes slightly clearer in the light of examples and of what Benveniste goes on to say about them. Always middle in Sanskrit and Greek – or deponent in Latin – are verbs meaning to be born, to lie or lay, to die (birth, copulation and death!), to grow, to speak and, significantly for our purposes, to imagine. In these cases, says Benveniste, 'the subject is the centre as well as the actor of the process; i.e. he accomplishes something which accomplishes itself in him, ... He is well and truly inside the process of which he is the agent'.

Passing to examples of verbs which admit of both active and middle forms, he contrasts the active *luei ton hippon*, he unties the horse, and the middle form *luetai ton hippon*, he unties the horse and in doing so affects himself (since as a result the horse is now his). The active form says the subject effects something. The middle form says the subject effects something and in so doing is affected himself.

Benveniste proposes that instead of the terms 'active voice' and 'middle voice' which suggest a less satisfying opposition than 'active voice' and 'passive voice', we mark the opposition with the terms 'external diathesis' and 'internal diathesis'. The expression 'internal diathesis' captures a part of the force of the middle voice as this is interpreted by Gonda, who, after a detailed survey of the evidence, concludes that

> the 'original' or 'essential' function of the medial voice was not exactly to signify that the subject 'performs a process that is performed in himself', but to denote that a process is taking place with regard to, or is affecting, happening to, a person or a thing; this definition includes also those cases in which we are under the impression that in the eyes of those who once used this category in its original function some power or something powerful was at work in or through the subject, or manifested itself in or by means of the subject on the one hand and those cases in which the process, whilst properly performed by, or originating with, the subject, obviously was limited to the 'sphere' or the subject.[10]

What Gonda means by limitation to the 'sphere' of the subject is illustrated by the difference between *louein*, to wash something, and *louesthai*, which refers to a person's washing himself or bathing. There need not be much effort expended on the part of

the person concerned. He may simply let himself into the water.
There need be no act of will such as is expressed by the active
verb *ethelo*; there need only be willingness as expressed by the
middle verb *boulomai* which comes from the same root.[11] Gonda
comes within an ace of reducing the middle voice to the passive.
He is drawn into this by his understandable desire to explain
why so many verbs one might expect to be medial are in fact
active in form. His explanation turns on the generally accepted
idea that languages have tended to lose the medial forms and
replace them (either with passives or) with personal active forms
as man came to see himself more as the master of a desacralised
environment. He speculates that active forms which one might
have expected to be medial, for example, Greek or Sanskrit verbs
for 'to fear', 'to be hungry', 'to blow' (of the wind) and 'to suffer'
(!) derive from impersonal forms contemporary with a pre-
technological, animist mentality. This explanation appears to
have induced him to assimilate the medials to the impersonal
forms like *es regnet*, *es donnert* and . . . *es gibt*, there is.

The Greek *esti* (Sanskrit *asti*), to be, and *eimi*, I am, are active,
but *esomai*, I shall be, is medial.[12] This, Gonda suggests,

> may be associated with, and partly explained from, wide-
> spread and fundamental habits of thought, which have tended
> to prevent man from acquiring . . . a modern command of the
> fundamental conception of time, involving recognition of the
> ideas of before and after, past, present, and future, in the
> sequence of events . . . time is not regarded as a straight line,
> as a regular succession of single and irrevocable moments, but
> as duration or as periodical recurrence . . . This category (the
> middle voice) allows the speaker to observe a certain *reserve*
> with regard to the part of the subject in a process which
> belongs to the future, to be guarded in his statements of the
> future activity or initiative of himself, his interlocutors or
> other people . . . About the future man can never and nowhere
> be completely certain; the time which will come hereafter is
> vaguely filled with possibilities . . .

Consider now the following passage from Derrida:

> 'difference' could be said to designate the productive and
> primordial constituting causality, the process of scission and

division whose differings and differences would be the prod-
ucts or constituted effects. But while bringing us closer to the
infinitive and active core of differing, 'differance' (with an *a*)
neutralises what the infinitive denotes as simply active, in the
same way that 'mouvance' does not signify in our language the
simple fact of moving, of moving oneself or of being moved.
Nor is resonance the act of resounding. Here in the usage of
our language we must reflect on the fact that the ending -*ance*
is undecided *between* active and passive. And we shall see why
that which lets itself [*se laisse*] be designated by 'differance' is
neither simply active nor simply passive, but announces or
rather recalls something like the middle voice, that it speaks of
an operation which is not an operation, which lets itself [*se
laisse*] be .thought neither as a passion nor as an action of a
subject upon an object, neither as departing from [*à partir de*;
cp. Benveniste's formulation of the middle voice quoted above]
an agent nor from a patient, neither from nor with a view to
any of these *terms*. Now perhaps philosophy, constituting itself
within this repression, began by hiving off into the active or
the passive voice a certain non-transitivity, the middle voice.
[*M* 9 (9), *SP* 137]

The main object of Derrida's comparison of differance and the
middle voice is to point to what exceeds the contrast between the
active and the passive [*BSF* 120]. There is a remnant of this
excess in the German word *lassen*, meaning both to let and to get,
for example to get someone to do something. Heidegger's *Gelas-
senheit* and *Seinlassen*, letting be, preserve this force. So does
Derrida's 'differance', except that he wishes to indicate that the
ontological force of Heidegger's words is the resultant of a force
that exceeds ontology. Still, the towardness stressed in Heidegger's rethinking of Husserl's account of the relationship of protention and retention is reflected in the deferring of Derrida's
differance, its deference or, to use the word which both he and
Gonda employ, reserve.

This middle voice of differance is not a mean between the
active and passive, a halfway house, part active, part passive. Its
milieu is, as we have already been advised, not a coincidence of
opposites. If it were it would not be an undecidable, but a
decided third value. We know too that the 'a' of differance marks
the temporisation which supplements the alterity of difference

(with an 'e') and the polemical distancing, *espacement, Ent-fernung*, which holds the alternands together in their altercation. Hence the milieu is not just place or space or *chôra*. It is space timed and time spaced. Via a forced marriage of the Greek *diapherein* and the Latin *differre*, a hymeneal dissemination, Derrida is trying to construe the proto-syntax of the locus which is also *mouvance*, the locomotive necessary condition of the possibility of the space of the classical logic of identity and of the dialectical negation which Hegel claimed to be the motivating condition of the necessity of the concept. The middle voice, milieu, *entre, antre*, hymen, differance, dissemination, call it what you will, is also proto-semantic. 'Its semantic void *signifies*, but it signifies spacing and articulation; it has as its meaning the possibility of syntax; it orders the play of meaning. *Neither purely syntactic nor purely semantic*, it marks the articulated opening of the opposition' [*Diss* 251–2 (222)]. Before rereading this text in the context of post-Fregean semiology, we shall pause to take note of a Freudian text of which 'La Double séance', its author tells us, proposes a rereading. This may help us to understand better why Derrida says that ' "Undecidability" is not caused here by some enigmatic equivocality, some inexhaustible ambivalence of a word in a "natural" language, and still less by some "*Gegensinn der Urworte*" (Abel)' [*Diss* 249 (220)].

III INSIDEOUTNESS

In his paper 'Das Unheimliche' ('The Uncanny')[13] Freud speculates on the following entries in Grimm's dictionary, a work to which Heidegger has frequent recourse, under *Heimlich*, a word to whose opposite Heidegger resorts no less frequently: '*Heimlich*, also in the sense of a place free from ghostly influences . . . familiar, friendly, intimate.' '*Heimlich* in a different sense, as withdrawn from knowledge, unconscious: . . . *Heimlich* also has the meaning of that which is obscure, inaccessible to knowledge.' Thus, Freud infers, the notion of 'something hidden and dangerous' is developed to the point where *heimlich* comes to mean what is usually meant by *unheimlich*: 'Thus *heimlich* is a word the meaning of which develops towards an ambivalence, until it finally coincides with its opposite, *unheimlich*. *Unheimlich* is in some way or other a sub-species of *heimlich*.' The *unheimlich* is 'in some way or other' in the *heimlich*, as Derrida finds Heidegger saying at those moments when he has intimations of the anasemiological pressure that solicits the fundamental semiology of being. This would explain why Jentsch should think that the essence of uncanniness is the sense of not knowing where one is, 'intellectual uncertainty'. Freud however believes that this analysis is inadequate and that it calls for completion by the idea that the feeling of uncanniness is experienced when there is a revival of something once familiar which has been repressed, for example an infantile castration complex or womb phantasy or the notion that one can bring about an event, such as someone's death, simply by willing it. That is, 'the prefix "un" is the mark of repression.'

Nine years before publishing 'Das Unheimliche' Freud published a review of Karl Abel's 'The Antithetical Sense of Primal Words'.[14] Examples of German words with antithetical sense are the 'speculative' words cited by Hegel. Another example is Heidegger's *Ent-schlossenheit*, where the hyphen marks the idea of openness or disclosure which gets covered over by the idea of closure conveyed by the word *Entschlossenheit* and the word 'resoluteness' which English translators of Heidegger commonly use for this. Another example from Heidegger is *Ent-fernung*, meaning both distancing and de-distancing. Abel mentions examples from German, but it is the antithetical words of Ancient Egyptian that give him particular delight.

> Now in the Egyptian language, this sole relic of a primitive world, there are a fair number of words with two meanings, one of which is the exact opposite of the other. Let us suppose, if such an obvious piece of nonsense can be imagined, that in German the word 'strong' meant both 'strong' and 'weak'; that in Berlin the noun 'light' was used to mean both 'light' and 'darkness'; that one Munich citizen called beer 'beer', while another used the same word to speak of water: this is what the astonishing practice amounts to which the ancient Egyptians regularly followed in their language. How could anyone be blamed for shaking his head in disbelief?

In view of the advanced state of Egyptian civilisation Abel dismisses the thought that this feature of the Egyptian language can be put down to a low level of mental development; and he rules out explanation in terms of a chance similarity of sound. Nor will such explanations do for a still more perplexing feature of the Egyptian lexicon:

> quite apart from the words that combine antithetical mean-
> ings, it possesses other compound words in which two vo-
> cables of antithetical meanings are united so as to form a
> compound which bears the meaning of only one of its constitu-
> ents. Thus in this extraordinary language there are not only
> words meaning equally 'strong' or 'weak', and 'command' or
> 'obey', but there are also compounds like 'old-young', 'far-
> near', 'bind-sever', 'outside-inside' . . . which, in spite of com-
> bining the extremes of difference, mean only 'young', 'near',
> 'bind' and 'inside' respectively . . .

That is, Ancient Egyptian has apparently bipolar words with monopolar sense and apparently monopolar words with bipolar sense. But for both of these features Abel offers a single explanation, namely that every concept is the twin of its opposite, so that the language can be expected to have *etyma* that commemorate this opposition. For example, the difference between 'strong' and 'weak' will be expressed by introducing a picture of one kind or another alongside the undifferentiated word 'strongweak' to determine which of the opposite senses is intended. Later the rootword *ken* will undergo modification to *kan* which will now mean weak while *ken* now means strong. Abel cites Bain: 'If everything that we can know is viewed as a transition from something else, experience must have two sides; and either every name must have a double meaning, or else for every meaning there must be two names'.[15]

While refusing to accept some of Abel's theories, Freud is sufficiently impressed by Abel's pamphlet to declare that it was not until he chanced to read it that he understood what he had written at least ten years before in *The Interpretation of Dreams* about the curious tendency of the dream-work to ignore the word 'No' and to represent contraries by a single element 'so that there is no way of deciding at first glance whether any element that admits of a contrary is present in the dream-thoughts as a positive or as a negative'. This statement tells us why Derrida cannot accept what Bain and Abel say as an explanation of what he himself is trying to say about undecidability – at least if Freud is justified in accepting what Abel says as an explanation of what he had been trying to say a decade or so before. Freud says 'there is no way of deciding at first glance'. Derrida says there is no way of deciding at second glance either. In fact, the more careful and sustained one's scrutiny, the worse confusion becomes confounded. Hegel was wrong when he wrote 'This double use of language, which gives to the same word a positive and negative meaning . . . gives no ground for reproaching language as a cause of confusion.' Though he was right to say it was no accident.[16]

Further, Abel's undecidables have about them the neutrality and indifference of Schelling's constructive identity. There is no place for the *labour* of the negative, let alone the labour of deconstructive differance. Although many of Derrida's chiasmic constructs may seem to spread their weight equally over their two feet, he would recommend as a useful mnemonic the happy chance that the Greek character *chi* extends one leg slightly further than the other [*Pos* 95 (70), *VEP* 189]. *Pas* is both the *pas* of negativity, and the *pas* of transgression, the *pas de marche*, and *marche* is step as well as stop or limit: it is limit de-limited, *plus de limite*, no more limit as well as more limit, mark (*horos*) and de-marcation. *Plus de métaphore, plus de jalousie, plus de pas, plus de noms, plus de plus* [*M* 261 (219), *Pas* 150, *Glas* 229, *Diss* 307 (274)]. Derrida and Nietzsche would agree with Freud that the prefix 'un' may often mark repression. Although Derrida's *enseignement* is how to undo things with words and how things and words undo themselves, the 'method', the theory, the practice and the process are not ultimately negative. This is why, although he lingers over the uncanny, indeed terrifying, fashion in which appropriation spawns impropriation or expropriation from inside itself [*OA* 153, *S(C)* 150, *Ja* 99, *Pas* 170], he sometimes classifies this process as de-propriation [*S (C)* 146], if one can speak of classifying such an unspeakable monstrosity. The explication of this *supplément de noeud, supplément de ne, supplement of (k)not* [*ECM* 40] is *de*-nouement. Chapter 7 and the Post-script treat of classification and the monstrosity of what is undecidably neither just one thing nor just the other and yet both. By way of anticipation it will be timely to end this chapter by warning that the kind of denouement to be expected from Derrida is not to be confused with the kind of which the following is an example from Hume:

Natural may be opposed, either to what is *unusual, miraculous*, or *artificial*. In the two former senses, justice and property are undoubtedly natural. But as they suppose reason, forethought, design, and social union and confederacy among men, perhaps that epithet cannot strictly, in the last sense, be applied to them.[17]

Justice is neither natural nor artificial yet both, if you choose and
confuse your senses carefully or carelessly enough. When you make
certain distinctions however you shed light on how things stand.
But it is the very notion of distinction that Derrida deconstructs.
Deconstruction is not disambiguation. It is not semiological clarification. It is an anasemiological operation that only makes clear the
limits of clarification. Derrida's demonstration, with regard, for
example, to Rousseau in the second part of *De la grammatologie*, that
writing, education and masturbation cannot be simply opposed as
artificial surrogates to 'undoubtedly natural' speaking, life and
sexual intercourse, but are strangely of their essence, falls short of
his purpose if it fails to bring out what makes ambiguity and
equivocity possible (as effect) and impossible (as anything more
than effect). Derrida is not accusing Rousseau of faulty logic. The
fault is in logic, not just in Rousseau. It is a structural fault. The
faute is an *il faut*, a necessity. Rousseau's 'dangerous supplement'
[*G* 203ff. (141ff.)], in its different forms of culture, writing and
disseminative onanism, is a form of the originary supplementarity
that makes form possible and impossible.

> In the same way that the 'fatal advantage' of sexual auto-
> affection begins well before what is thought to be circum-
> scribed by the name of masturbation (organization of so-called
> wrong and pathological gestures, confined to some children or
> adolescents), the supplementary menace of writing is older than
> what some think to exalt by the name of 'speech.'
>   From then on, metaphysics consists of excluding non-presence
> by determining the supplement as *simple exteriority*, pure addition
> or pure absence. The work of exclusion operates within the
> structure of supplementarity. The paradox is that one annuls
> addition by considering it a pure addition. *What is added is nothing*
> *because it is added to a full presence to which it is exterior.* Speech comes
> to be added to intuitive presence (of the entity, of *essence*, of the
> *eidos*, of *ousia*, and so forth); writing comes to be added to living
> self-present speech; masturbation comes to be added to so-called
> normal sexual experience; culture to nature, evil to innocence,
> history to origin, and so on.
>   The concept of origin or nature is nothing but the myth of
> addition, of supplementarity annulled by being purely additive.
> It is the myth of the effacement of the trace, that is to say of an
> originary differance that is neither absence nor presence, neither

negative nor positive. Originary differance is supplementary as *structure*. Here structure means the irreducible complexity within which one can only shape or shift the play of presence or absence: that within which metaphysics can be produced but which metaphysics cannot think. [*G* 237–8 (167)]

Supplementarity is the danger *of* logocentrism. Logocentrism's danger. Instead of resolving, like Hume, an apparent surface contradiction between two terms by making explicit an ambiguity in them, Derrida brings out a deep structural 'contradiction' by making explicit an ambivalence in the superficially oppositive relation between the terms, an ambivalence for which his markers are the catachreses 'supplement', *'pharmakon'*, 'hymen', 'differance', 'writing', 'spacing', 'trace' and so on.

7   The Divided Line

How differently to Lueli was he taking his loss. The reason must be that Lueli though losing his god had kept his faith. Lueli had lost something real, like losing his umbrella; he had lost it with frenzy and conviction. But *his* loss was utter and retrospective, a lightning-flash loss which had wiped out a whole life-time of having. In fact the best way of expressing it was to say that what he had lost for ever was nothing. 'Forever is a word that stretches backward too,' he explained to himself. If any proof were needed his own behaviour was supplying it. He had ceased to believe in God, but this was making no difference to him. Consequently what he had ceased to believe in had never been.

Sylvia Townsend Warner, *Mr Fortune's Maggot*

I   THE SOFTNESS OF THE LOGICAL MUST

Presentation or public practice. Ostension or institution. It is natural to suppose that it is one or the other of these alternatives that is the bedrock of meaning. Whether semiological rock-bottom is the one or the other or both is the topic of a debate that was already underway with Cratylus and is underway still after Frege, Russell and Wittgenstein. Presentational theories are of two kinds, private and public. It is an open question whether the *parousia* Wittgenstein posits in the *Tractatus* is private or public. That is a question that seems not to interest him there. *Parousia* goes public only in the *Blue Book* where the task formerly attributed to ostension neutrally described is transferred to criteria and rules.[1] But the identification of criteria depends on more or less direct *deixis*, phenomenological demonstration. In the *Philosophical Investigations* and the *Remarks on the Foundations of Mathematics* the assumption of more or less rigid designation that both the private and the public analyses assume is replaced by a

semiology restricted to the description of language games and
forms of life, a semiology which, as Heidegger would say, sees
sense and reference as primarily forms of handiness, *Zuhanden-
heit*, *Handlung* and *praxis* rather than of presentation and representation. The given is not a simple datum of sense, whether a
sensation, a *sensatum* or a clear and distinct Cartesian or Husserlian *cogitatum*. I can be called upon to justify my use of a word,
and I may then produce a definition or point to criteria. But
these justificatory practices are practices, and they presuppose
words that are used without justification, though not without
right. 'To use a word without justification does not mean to use
it without right. What I do is not, of course, to identify my
sensations by criteria: but to repeat an expression.'[2] Ultimately
there is nothing more that I can do than affirm 'This language
game is played'. I have struck the stratum against which my
spade is turned. At this level there is no room for appeal to
anything more certain than the sureness of the practice which is
the condition of the possibility of theoretical certainty and doubt.
This is why in *On Certainty*, while unable to accept the proof of an
external world that Moore bases on his claim to know that there
exist two hands, those hands held up in front of his audience at
the British Academy lecture there and then on 22 November
1939 (*en ce moment même*), Wittgenstein does not take the sceptical
alternative. Plainly Moore and anyone else for whom bedrock is
assumed to be intuition or sensation is in competition with the
epistemological and semiological sceptic. Wittgenstein construes
foundations otherwise, in such a wise as to bring the philosopher
to see that it is not a live option whether they are objects of
knowledge or whether they are never more than objects of
sceptical doubt. Since no epistemological question about foundations is well-founded or well-formed, both the affirmation and
the denial of knowledge about them are misplaced. There can be
no proof from known premises of the sort Moore imagines he
produces; nor can there be doubt. And this does not mean that
we cannot know (tacitly?) what the foundations are about which
we cannot ask whether or not they themselves are bits of knowledge. Wittgenstein must know this in order to be able to tell us
what it is about which this question cannot properly be asked,
and in order to be in a position to deconstruct the philosophical
misconstrual and reconstrue otherwise, as the forms of life with
which we are all pretheoretically familiar.

Despite a widespread interpretation of his later work, Wittgenstein is never against foundations. He is against a philosophical picture of what they are, the picture that dictates the feeling that if knowledge is based on customary practice, the familiar forms of life, then, because custom is contingent, claims to knowledge must be acknowledged as a sham. Of course, there is a time-honoured objection to such scepticism according to which scepticism gets hoist with its own petard as soon as it claims for itself the status of knowledge and truth. This is why, like Wittgenstein, Derrida resists the suggestion that he is an anti-sceptic or a renovated Hume, supposing Hume was a philosophical sceptic, which Derrida doubts. Philosophical scepticism is internal to philosophy in that it claims for itself truth. It crashes its head against the limits of logic. If it is to get anywhere it must cease to be philosophical, become the senseless heir of philosophy that can totter no further than the threshold of sense, the nonlieu between the logic of the said and the rhetoric of saying [*BSF* 114–15, *M* 42(38)]. 'Scepticism is *refutable*, but it returns also to haunt us'.[3] Not just philosophical scepticism, but it together with its mongrel Doppelgänger of which we can use only the bastard kind of reasoning, to which Plato refers at *Timæus* 52b, and anasemiological double-talk.

But although neither Derrida nor Wittgenstein posit philosophical scepticism or its opposite, there is a menace of something *unheimlich*, something sinister, some Thing (*Chose terrifiante*) in the space between Derrida's lines akin to the *horror vacui* and the fear of madness that, under the threat of scepticism, lurk in the pages of the *Metaphysical Meditations*. The joke-work of Derrida's poetic prose is not a merely frivolous play upon words [*Fors* 21 (75)]. There is a serious question at stake, nothing less than the question of the unmeaning of Being. It would of course be grotesque to imply that metaphysical anxiety never haunts the later writings of Wittgenstein and that what one finds in its pages is always all sweetness and light. Here, in case anyone should consider it necessary, is just one piece of evidence to refute that staggering suggestion:

The problems arising through a misinterpretation of our forms of language have the character of *depth*. They are deep disquietudes; their roots are as deep in us as the forms of our language and their significance is as great as the importance of our language. — Let us ask ourselves: why do we feel a grammatical joke to be *deep*? (And that is what the depth of philosophy is.)[4]

Even so, the cracks through to these depths are trimly papered over by Wittgenstein's idea that philosophy is put to rest if we keep within the limits of the forms of life in which language is at home. It is on and in this *Heimlichkeit* that Wittgenstein's later work dwells. Whereas Derrida, although not a philosophical sceptic about truth, names and concepts, is continually contriving to prevent us forgetting that these are but semiological *effects*, stage effects and staged effects *per*formed by anasemiological differance [*ECM* 47], so the performance is never *the* performance, never the first night. It is always re-hearsal, *répétition*. As Derrida puts it in 'Freud and the Scene of Writing', referring to the effect's cause (*causa, chose*, thing) as force (which is *fors*, outside, as well as *for*, inside, from *forum*, market and meeting place, *ting, Ding*, thing):

Force produces meaning (and space) through the power of 'repetition' alone, which inhabits it originally as its death. This power, that is, this lack of power, which opens and limits the labour of force, institutes translatability, makes possible what we call 'language', transforms an absolute idiom into a limit which is always already transgressed: a pure idiom is not language; it becomes so only through repetition; repetition always already divides the point of departure of the first time. [*ED* 316 (213)]

There never was any *once* upon a time. Although, as Saussure emphasised, language is a system of differences which permit semantic classification,

these differences *play*: in language, in speech too, and in the exchange between language and speech. On the other hand, these differences are themselves *effects*. They have not fallen from the sky fully formed, and are no more inscribed in a *topos noëtos*, than they are prescribed in the gray matter of the brain. If the word 'history' did not in and of itself convey the motif of a final repression of difference, one could say that only

differences can from the start of play be thoroughly 'historical'. [*M* 12 (11), *SP* 140–1; cp. *BSF* 104]

Part of Derrida's programme therefore is to find a middle way
between Frege, who denied that concepts are historical, and
Hegel, whose negatively dialectical account of the historicity of
concepts is one to which, as we have seen, Derrida cannot
subscribe. What position on this spectrum is occupied by the late
semiology of Wittgenstein?

Frege's semiology is synchronic like the linguistic science of
Saussure. This synchronism emerges again in Wittgenstein's
readiness to allow that sometimes when it may seem that we
have one concept in mind it would be better to say that there are
two, in which case we should do well to mark the difference by
using a different word. The question turns on the consequences
of using only one. It is the consequences that force us to think
there are two concepts rather than only one. The actual and
imagined consequences determine where we draw the line. What
the consequences are will depend on general facts of physical
and human nature. So what we find it necessary to think will be
marked by historical contingency. This historical contingency
does not mean that there cannot be a science of language which
sets out a taxonomy of its concepts. Like Saussure, we can
abstract from the events which cause a linguistic system to change,
and regard these as events which affect the system from outside,
like foreign bodies which disturb the order of a galactic system.
This is Saussure's analogy, and it would seem to be one to which
Frege too might appeal. The concepts whose non-historical nature
he is at pains to affirm are those of arithmetical systems, but his
view of these is an expression of a view of concepts in general, in
particular the view that sense must be determinate. Hence he
objects to Peano's readiness to admit piecemeal, conditional
definitions, for instance of '+', first defining it for integers, then
for fractions, then for numbers which are irrational or complex.
Although in practice we may have to make do with definitions
that are 'transitive', as Payne Knight and Dugald Stewart would
say, these should be treated as transitory, on the way to the
single definition that logic demands for each sign.[5] This is a
demand that Wittgenstein makes in the *Tractatus*. It is aban-
doned in the *Philosophical Investigations* and the *Remarks on the
Foundations of Mathematics*. There formal logic and arithmetic turn

out to depend for their sense on non-formal practices employing signs that permit no final definition, on regularities of institutional behaviour that rule out the formulation of an ultimate ruling. Siding with Peano against Frege, Wittgenstein now says: 'we extend our concept of number as in spinning a thread we twist fibre on fibre'.[6] This does not mean that our concepts are utterly arbitrary. 'Compare a concept with a style of painting. For is even our style of painting arbitrary? Can we choose one at pleasure? (The Egyptian, for instance.)'[7] 'The rules of grammar may be called "arbitrary", if that is to mean that the *aim* of the grammar is nothing but that of the language.'[8] Arbitrariness of this kind does not exclude logical necessity. It requires only that we break away from a familiar philosophical concept of necessity – and of the wish, the proposition, the thought, the concept:

> A wish seems already to know what will or would satisfy it; a proposition, a thought, what makes it true – even when that thing is not there at all! Whence this *determining* of what is not yet there? This despotic demand? ('The hardness of the logical must.')[9]

The logical must has a soft centre. Is not this what Derrida also is saying? For example when, although insisting on the aleatory character of text, he insists that chance plays within a context of necessity: 'the expression "passivity more passive than passivity" does not become whatever you please; it does not mean "activity more active than activity" ' [*ECM* 47]; 'the word "work" has no more than any other a fixed sense outside the mobile syntax of its marks, outside contextual transformation. The variation is not free, the transformation is regulated, in its irregularity and its very derangement' [*ECM* 51]. But, he goes on to ask ominously, 'By what? By whom?' As though to question the stark opposition between *effet de hasard* and *procédé conscient* made in Saussure's research into the anagrams of proper names which, according to him, certain Latin poets secreted in their verse. There is a striking similarity (whether a chance effect or a conscious operation I cannot say) between what Derrida writes and what Starobinski writes when the latter suggests that we reject the opposition in favour of the idea that the anagram is an aspect of a process which is neither purely fortuitous nor fully conscious.

Why might there not be an iteration, a generative verbal repetition [palilalia], which would project and redouble in what is
said the materials of a first word which was neither uttered nor
kept back? In spite of not being a conscious *rule*, the anagram
may nevertheless be considered a *regularity* (or a law) where
the arbitrariness of the theme word entrusts itself to the
necessity of a process.[10]

'Process' (*processus*) here needs handling with care, but in its relation
to 'chance effect' and 'conscious operation' it may be Starobinski's
attempt to express that for which Derrida invokes the middle voice.
'Theme word' could also mislead us with regard to Derrida's theory
and practice, as I shall try to bring out later on. Meanwhile, I
am content if I have shown that Derrida and Wittgenstein (and
Starobinski) are united by an endeavour to analyse the economy
(restricted or general) of an exchange between necessity and
chance. United, but polemically, as too with other post-Fregean
philosophers – and certain Pre-Socratics.

To confirm this, is it not to what Derrida would call a
'structural' possibility that Wittgenstein is pointing when, devel-
oping Peano's reflections on defining '+', he puts it to us that no
rule prescribing, for example, 'Add 2' can be determinate enough
to proscribe a series beginning 2, 4, 6, 8 . . . , but including a
subsequent sequence like 28, 44, 76, and so on, whatever 'and so
on' may here mean? Is not 'Add 2' a structural undecidable? For
it is as well satisfied by 2, 4, 6, 8, 12, 18, . . . as by 2, 4, 6, 8, 10,
12, 14, ... There is no telling whether 'Add 2', as we understand it, prohibits a sequence like (like? How like?) 8, 12, 18, . . .
('Madd 2'). It is no good saying that the undecidability is purely
theoretical and that which is the correct kind of progression is
settled by looking at what we do in practice. For the nature of
what we do in practice, what it is that we do, how we go on in
fact, implies that we can spell out the 'and so on'. And it is the
open texture of this that gives rise to the undecidability. True,
this observation will not worry Wittgenstein. He will continue to
recommend that, instead of just thinking, we should look, and
look again when we have waited long enough to be able to discover
an advantage which is enjoyed by going on in this way rather than
that; never mind that we can be taught what 'this way' and what
'that way' mean only by ostension – which is the real 'Wittgenstein
Paradox': that after moving from a semiology modelled on osten-

sion to one based on use where meaning includes the point of a practice, we should be able to distinguish practices only by pointing.

The pointing that identifies a practice and distinguishes one practice from another is an explanation of the 'and so on'.[11] What is pointed to is a customary use or *praxis* ,[12] whether a communal practice or the practice of a single person that is in principle capable of becoming communal. But the only way someone can point to what one generally does is to point to what particular people do in particular circumstances, for example, when asked to explain what a certain expression means. That, according to Wittgenstein, is all there is to the explanation of meaning: 'if you want to understand the use of the word "meaning", look for what are called "explanations of meaning" '.[13] No further 'fact of the matter' is required. Here Wittgenstein and Derrida are at one. Both aim to dissipate the charm of the picture of meaning as a representation, here and now before the private eye or ear of the mind or deposited in a public archive, so potent that every permissible employment of an expression with that meaning is preordained, already signed, sealed and delivered. Wittgenstein and Derrida are agreed that what is permissible is what will turn out (*se trouve*: 'an idiom hesitating between chance and necessity')[14] to be permissible and that what turns out to be permissible is identified by what is permitted. Not that what any particular person permits settles what is permissible. Nothing and nobody settles anything once and for all. Some permissions carry more weight than others. But which do is something else that turns out and hesitates between chance and necessity; and between chance as hazard, risk, ill-fortune (*méchance*) and chance as good luck or opportunity (*mes chances*).[15]

Here Derrida reaches 'a point of almost absolute proximity' [*Pos* 60 (44)] to Wittgenstein where their difference is hardly more than a difference of rhetorical emphasis. Both question the idea that the rule of semantic law calls for a formula or algorithm that takes care of all its applications by representing and prepresenting them in a here and now that remotely controls future moves in the language game as a piston rod determines movements in other parts of a machine, these moves, like these movements, being calculable in advance. They agree that a law does not represent what is legal in this way, for a law is not thus representable. Let us 'cease representing law to ourselves, apprehending law itself under the species of the representable. Perhaps law itself outreaches any representation, perhaps it is never before us, as what posits itself in a figure or composes a figure for itself . . . perhaps the law itself manages to do no more than transgress the figure of all possible representation.'[16] Perhaps the *Gesetz*, that which lays down what is laid down, cannot be laid down, posited, *gesetzt*. A form of words can be proposed, but precisely what those words prohibit and permit is postponed *sine die*. What a rule rules in and rules out remains to be seen. Forever, if the precision we are looking for is a precision that leaves no room for judgement, that stops up all cracks.[17] Forever, even if the precision we seek is no more than what is sufficient for a particular purpose.[18] There is need to spell out a rule only where the need arises to exclude a specific misunderstanding. No amount of spelling out will exclude every conceivable risk. And however much or however little we spell out a rule, the spelling out sooner or later comes down to rules that are followed without being represented, rules that are followed blindly.[19]

Both Wittgenstein and Derrida investigate the play of necessity and chance. But what Wittgenstein stresses is that all necessity is not lost when we abandon the piston rod picture of semantic necessity. He is addressing himself to those who feel nervous without this idea, and administers consolation. Whereas Derrida's remarks are addressed to those whose confidence in this idea has not yet been shaken. He concentrates on what corresponds to the first part of the task Wittgenstein sets himself in his later work. However, it must be remembered that the first part of Derridian deconstruction, in which an old order of precedence between opposites is reversed, is complemented by a second stage in which it is shown that each term of a classical opposition involves and is involved with the other. And whereas the second part of Wittgenstein's programme tenders recompense and solace, the second part of Derrida's programme is no less discomforting than the first. Admittedly, the disillusioned may find comfort in the thought that Derrida is not denying that there are semantic effects. But Derrida will not let him forget that they are only effects and that among other effects are notions of contrast, difference and limit that do not stand up to scrutiny: for example the contrasts between the different and the same and the limit between chance and necessity. If we look closely at these oppositions – *too* closely, Wittgenstein would say – their terms turn out to be indeterminate, undecidables.

II. DESTINERRANCE

Another at least apparent undecidable, a close relation to the Wittgenstein case just examined, is whether 'green' excludes 'blue' or is compatible with it as it would be in the circumstance that it means 'grue', that is to say 'before time *t* green but after *t* blue', neither alternative being less likely and less lawlike than the other.[20] Nelson Goodman thinks this is not a real undecidable. He argues that a conflict between interpretative hypotheses both of which are in principle equally legitimate is to be resolved by choosing the one that has become entrenched in practice: 'to the question what distinguishes those recurrent features of experience that underlie valid projections from those that are not, I am suggesting that the former are those features for which we have adopted predicates that we have habitually projected.'[21] Having made it clear that an unfamiliar predicate can be entrenched and a familiar one not deeply entrenched, that, as he puts it, 'Entrenched capital, in protecting itself, must yet allow full scope for free enterprise', he asks:

> Are we not trusting too blindly to a capricious Fate to see to it that just the right predicates get themselves comfortably entrenched? Must we not explain why, in cases of conflict like those illustrated, the really projectible predicate happens to have been the earlier and more often projected? And in fact wasn't it projected so often *because* its projection was so often obviously legitimate, so that our proposal begs the question?

In the course of answering himself Goodman says that entrenchment is a sufficient but not necessary indication of projectibility. Now it must be granted that saying something is a sufficient indication is not the same as saying that it is a sufficient condition. However, it is not easy to grasp what Goodman can mean by a necessary indication unless he means a necessary condition, in which case it is probable that he is contrasting it with a sufficient condition. If this is what he means his statement is at

odds with his later statement, made in answer to the question
why projections of entrenched predicates are those which turn
out to be true, that we do not know whether they will turn out to
be true. We do not know, for instance, until the time comes,
whether all emeralds are green or grue. 'We have no guarantees.
The criterion for the legitimacy of projections cannot be truth
that is as yet undetermined.' This eminently sane remark concedes that capricious Fate does have a hand in what we mean,
concedes the softness of the logical must that coincides with
Derrida's *nécessité dure* [*OA* 153].

As Saul Kripke asks, administering another twist to the screw,
when time *t* comes, how do I know that when I said 'green' in the
past I didn't mean the same as 'grue'?

> If the *blue* object before me now is grue, then it falls in the
> extension of 'green', as I meant it in the past. It is no help to
> suppose that in the past I stipulated that 'green' was to apply
> to all and only those things 'of the same colour as' the sample.
> The sceptic can reinterpret 'same colour' as same *schmolor*,
> where things have the same schmolor if . . .[22]

Kripke makes this point in the context of the anti-behaviourist
assumption that I determine what I mean by a colour word by
imagining a mental sample. But appeal to purely public behavioural criteria does not eliminate indeterminacy, as we discovered
above. And as Quine has argued precisely on such a behavioural
assumption. The anthropologist cannot determine whether the
native speaker's 'gavagai' means rabbit, undetached rabbit part,
or rabbit stage, because he cannot determine whether another
expression the native speaker uses means 'means the same as' or
'belongs with'. And reference is infected by this undecidability,
because the English-speaking translator of Gavagese will be
unable to decide whether an expression of that exotic language is
a concrete general term like 'green' in 'The grass is green' or an
abstract singular term as in 'Green is a colour'. For there may be
systematic compensatory adjustments elsewhere in that language's equivalents of our English plural endings and definite
and indefinite articles. And does not the inscrutability encroach
upon our own language? 'Reference would seem now to become
nonsense not just in radical translation but at home.'[23]

There is thus no fact of the matter (not even the done thing, for the same indeterminacy frustrates any attempt to determine what that is) that determines what a word means or refers to, whether one's theory of sense and reference be cast in terms of private ostension or in terms of public criteria. How then can one stem the tide of indeterminacy that threatens to envelope all language, making it possible for any word to mean anything and therefore nothing? By, suggests Quine, embracing the thesis of ontological relativity. If we ask what the word 'rabbit' means and refers to we presume a language as a going concern that enables us to say which sense of 'rabbit' we have in mind. And then we have answered our question. Unless a similar question is put about a word that figures in the answer to the first. But in practice this regress ends 'by acquiescing in our mother tongue and taking its words at face value'. More generally:

> it makes no sense to say what the objects of a theory are, beyond saying how to interpret or reinterpret that theory in another; . . . talk of subordinate theories *is* meaningful, but only relative to the background theory with its own primitively adopted and ultimately inscrutable ontology.[24]

As with Wittgenstein and Goodman, so with Quine: home base is practice. And although practice is ultimately inscrutable, cannot be ultimately thematised, a proposition to which Derrida willingly assents, Derrida is unwilling to say simply that what is inscrutable is ontology. To think that is to forget the disontological. It is to forget what, except for rare moments, is forgotten in the thinking of Heidegger. Heidegger's reminders of the forgetting of the meaning of being for the most part conceal the forgetting of what resists the categories of being, transcends the *transcendens* both of mediæval ontology and of fundamental ontology, and disseminates the semantic.

> When Heidegger . . . supposes, behind the Greek language itself, this Greek language said to have been forgotten, defaced, mistranslated by the Romans, when he supposes that behind the Greek language itself there is another language, unthought even for the Greeks in their language, he presupposes something as it were archi-originally intact which was already profoundly forgotten but immediately retrieved from oblivion by, for example, the aboriginal Greeks. Hence Heidegger's warning against interpreting his text as a nostalgic return to the

Greeks in the manner of a well-known German tradition.
Nevertheless, although it is not a question of returning to the
Greek language, one must presuppose at least something
absolutely forgotten which already dissimulates itself always
behind the Greek language, an archi-maternal language, a
grandmotherly language . . . that cannot be touched. [*OA*
151–2]

Now Quine's inscrutable ontology is such a *noli me tangere*, a virgin
mémé, the immaculate granny of all discourse, as is Goodman's
comfortably entrenched custom and Wittgenstein's language
game of which all we can say is that it is played. Notwithstanding
Quine's statement that 'it makes no sense to say what the objects of
a theory are, beyond saying how to interpret or reinterpret that
theory in another', which might easily be mistaken for what
Derrida means by 'intertextuality', and notwithstanding his
critique of the notion of meaning as a nucleus which might be the
object of a Cratylic pure proper name, the domesticity which
characterises the Cratylic natural language carries over to the
restricted economy of Quine's conventional background theory
that is also a practice; as also to Goodman's entrenched property, to Wittgenstein's and Sarl's forms of life, to Saussure's
phonological *langue*, to Husserl's ideal of phenomenological presence, to Hegel's concretely universal absolute idea; and to
Heidegger's matricially caring core the desire for which is not
foreign to Derrida.

The nucleus may be dreamed of as something we could not or
should not name, to which we could in principle, in the last
analysis, give at least a pro-name, It or Thou or He or She.
Post-Fregean philosophy, following Hegel's highway of despair
from the idea of punctual sense-certainty to the idea of absolute
system, has learned the hard way that that dream is a dream.
Having been persuaded that the name has meaning only in the
context of a sentence, it has gone on to teach that it has meaning
only in the context of an entire form of life. But the idea of the
nucleus lives on, not as only a centre but as the circumference
too. It is now the self-contained whole. Perhaps not the system
we inhabit, but a perfect whole of which we dream.

There is a relation to the intact nucleus that is pre-historical,
pre-original, that from which any desire whatsoever can consti-

tute itself. So the desire or the phantasm of the intact nucleus is irreducible, but *there is no* intact nucleus. I would oppose desire to necessity, *Ananke. Ananke* is that there is no intact nucleus, there is none, there never was one, and it is this that we want to forget, the forgetting that we want in a certain way to forget. It is not as though there is something [some thing] forgotten: what we want to forget is that there is nothing to forget, that there never was anything to forget. [*OA* 153].

Nothing like an umbrella that might be forgotten by the absent-minded Professor of Philosophy at Freiburg who wrote 'The Question of Being' ('On/Over the Line'), or like what was *really meant* by a Professor of Classical Philology at Basle when he wrote 'I have forgotten my umbrella' [*Spurs* 122ff., 143]. Nothing like the nothing that Pompey was so astonished to find in the arcanum of the Holy of Holies, but which announces, without pronouncing his name, the God that should be loved less than the Script of the Torah, lest direct contact drive us insane [*ED* 151 (102)].[25] Nothing but the 'pure exchange where nothing is exchanged, where there is nothing real but the movement of exchange which is nothing'.[26] The secret is that there is no secret; *rien au-delà.*[27]

Jew/Greek, Derrida is more Greek than Jew in his recognition of the sinister aspect of *Ananke* that holds the attention not only of Heraclitus, but of Plato and Cratylus as well. The double aspect of *Ananke*, its chiasmic force, consists, as its Latin name of *Necessitas* indicates, at one and the same time lawlessness and law, arbitrariness and motivation, inexplicable Fate (Goodman) and explanation, nonsense and sense. It is a 'hymen between chance and rule', 'a play of . . . contingency with law' [*Diss* 309 (277)]. This is the view of *ananke* that Derrida finds in Heraclitus and Nietzsche. So, incidentally, does Deleuze, but he does not find it in Mallarmé who, he maintains, ascribes a represssive role to the rule.[28] Derrida, on the other hand, sees Heraclitean innocence and Nietzschean gaiety in Mallarmé's throw of the die. The two readings in question correspond roughly to two readings to be distinguished in Plato. In the Myth of Er in the *Republic*, *ananke* is the rule of law and order. In the *Timæus* it is errant force, the principle of uncertainty, the principle of unprincipledness that is Plato's gloss on the *apeiron* of Pythagoras. But in A. E. Taylor's opinion, 'If we want to grasp the meaning of

114   *Derrida on the Threshold of Sense*

Timæus, we must not take *ananke* to represent anything inherently lawless and irrational, and yet we must not take the word to mean necessity in the sense of conformity to law'.[29] And elsewhere:

> the Necessity of the *Timæus* is something quite different from the Necessity of the Myth of Er, or of the Stoics, which are personifications of the principle of rational law and order. On the other hand, Necessity is plainly not meant to be an independent, evil principle, for it is plastic to intelligence; mind 'for the most part' is said to 'persuade it'; its function is to be instrumental to the purposes of *nous*. The reason for introducing it into the story seems to be simply that it is impossible in science to resolve physical reality into a complex of rational laws without remainder.[30]

Here Taylor not only describes the supplementary 'logic' of *ananke*; he also refers to the 'remainder' which is unpersuaded by Platonic *nous*, recalcitrant to the Kantian category and left behind by Hegelian *Aufhebung*: the thing that is not possessed, the thing that is not [*Ja* 98–9, *OA* 101], the *cause-chose* that is the cause of Derrida's deep disquietude and explains why the desire he opposes to *ananke* is a hankering 'without hope for hope'.[31]

III   'THE MOST SHOCKING THING ABOUT DERRIDA'S WORK'

It is worth remembering that it is of all people Plato who (in the *Republic*) speaks of the shifting realm of the between and (in the *Cratylus*) devotes page after page to the kind of thing that Richard Rorty and the rest of us find most shocking about Derrida's work: 'multilingual puns, joke etymologies, allusions from anywhere, and phonic and typographical gimmicks'.[32] This thought may give pause to anyone inclined to pooh-pooh those pages of Derrida that draw on texts that are deemed so fancifully literary that they cannot deserve to be taken seriously by a philosopher worth his salt. Texts like those of Mallarmé.

In an essay on Mallarmé's *Coup de dés* Hyppolite writes of 'chance which turns itself into necessity in abolishing itself as chance'.[33] This sounds like an anticipation of Deleuze's interpre-

tation of Mallarmé. But both Deleuze and Hyppolite are aware
that Mallarmé's full title is *Un Coup de dés jamais n'abolira le hasard*:
'A throw of dice will never abolish chance'. Since we have been
primed not to assume that a title states the author's belief, we
may take into account also that under the title *Quant au livre*
Mallarmé writes, very much *à propos*:

Cette pratique —

Appuyer, selon la page, au blanc, qui l'inaugure son ingénuité, à
soi, oublieuse même du titre qui parlerait trop haut: et, quand
s'aligna, dans une brisure la moindre, disséminé, le hasard
vaincu mot par mot, indéfectiblement le blanc revient, tout à
l'heure gratuit, certain maintenant, pour conclure que rien
au-delà et authentiquer le silence —

True, we have been primed not to assume either that what
appears under a title states the author's belief, and this will be
especially risky with what is 'fancifully literary'. Still, we cannot
overlook the fact that Mallarmé writes: 'chance vanquished
word by word, indefectibly the blank returns'. Derrida does not
overlook this. Having recourse to Mallarmé – and to Ponge and
to Blanchot and to Genet and to Nietzsche and to Saussure . . . and
finally and first to Heraclitus [*BSF* 115] – he tries to steer a course
between opposing black to blank white and positing a neutral
grey. An example of such false opposition is that between so-
called natural languages and logico-mathematical formalisa-
tion. As we have seen, when Gödel proves unprovability the
undecidable becomes a decided grey third value. And when
Russell ejects paradoxicality from the metalanguage at the back
door by stipulating a theory of types, he lets arbitrariness in at
the front. He thus provides us with confirmation of the logic of
supplementarity that structures the very opposition between the
so-called natural and the so-called artificial. Perhaps the so-
called natural language is more successful at marking the formal
structure of undecidability than the formalised *Begriffsschrift*.
'Natural' language is less coy about exposing itself as 'unnatural'
writing, *pharmakon*.

The undecidability of the graphical structure of the Derridian
stroke between literature and philosophy (the relationship between
poetry and thinking that provoked the thinking of Heidegger

and the poetry-thinking of his *Gedachtes*) is fatally captured in the typographical structure of *Glas*. In the original edition (the paperback edition is different) both recto and verso of the volume's fold (*brisure*) are two parallel columns of which the one on the left is largely a crochet work of texts from Hegel plus running commentary, predominantly on the topics of genealogy, generality and gender. The same topics, among others, arise on the 'rectal' side of each page, where the texts most generously cited are from Genet, particularly ones concerning his family and the mother who gave him his name. While the Genet column is maternal and *weiblich*, the other, still genet-ic, stands for paternal truth. Each column is a phallus, male or female, and the columns are polemically united by Nietzsche's question of the genealogical relationship of truth as woman to truth as man. The hymeneal (dis)connection of the columns is complicated by the fact that Genet is marked by the undecidability of homosexuality. And this genealogical reading is crossed with a logical one, as the French *lit* is both bed and read, legend, *logos* [*Diss* 252 (222)]. The cleft between the pages and the white space between the columns is the copulative 'is' between the subject and predicate. Yet another fold in the manifold graphic of the hymen is produced by occasional slots of *wissenschaftlich* prose between the beds of 'flowery' language to the right and of poetry and personal letters between the scholarly paragraphs to the left.

All this Alexandrian fixing in order to postpone the fixing of *between*. But the purely syntactic between is not sufficiently taxic. It is too slow for words. It gets overtaken by the semantic. To its syncategorematic function categorematic meanings accrue. 'It can be nominalized, turn into a quasi-categorem, receive a definite article, or even be made plural' [*Diss* 251 (222)]. When it comes, instead of hymen, to be a count[34] noun it suffers the fate of Kant's schema when this, instead of being what Starobinski's *processus* is supposed to mark, the middle-voiced function performed by the productive imagination, it sediments into a part-sensory, part-conceptual quasi-image, no longer an enigma. There is much to recommend interpreting some of Derrida's writings as a reworking of Kant's analysis of the productive imagination *à partir de* Heidegger's reworking. That Derrida expresses a low estimation of the explanatory power of appeals to the imagination goes some way to confirm this. And when Derrida writes of God's 'discheminative' deconstruction of the

Tower that the Shemites have built, who is to gainsay that he is
alluding to the construction of the Kantian schema? [*OA* 137].
The dissemination of the schema will call for a shaking of the
confidence we put in a cover-all, cover-up concept of production.
This will need to be shifted in the direction of a certain impro-
duction which is not just the negation of production and which
does not belong to a conservative economy of memory and time
[*Ja* 89ff., *Diss* 328 (296)]. This does not mean a denial of memory
and temporality any more than it means a denial of production.
It means rather the excession of memory and time which opens
up the phenomenological time of living memory and expectation
to a time with a past that was never present and a future that will
never be produced. Phenomenological time is the time of Husserlian retention and protention and of Hegelian history. It is
also the time of the form(ation) of concepts which Wittgenstein
likens to the overlapping strands in a rope; and it is for this
reason that the historical risk which, against Frege, Wittgenstein
makes a grammatical property of conceptual open texture, the
historical risk and chance to which a concept is opened through
the judgement, wit and *Witze* with which the concept is applied
by the social imagination, admits a genealogicality that is closer
to the historicity of Hegel than to the 'historicity' of Derrida's
deferring. If we seek a neighbour of this last, one will be found in
Freud's notion of supplementation (*Nachträglichkeit*). According
to this the so-called primal scene may never have been witnessed
by the child, but is retrospectively constituted as an act of
parental intercourse when the child is mature enough to repeat
the phantasy in an appropriately structured dream. The so-
called primal scene is secondary. It becomes a traumatic cause
(for instance of anxiety) through being made into one by an
after-effect.

Now a somewhat similar temporal structure is to be found in
what Kant says about threefold synthesis.[35] If Kant is right in
saying that there can be no initial perception, no apprehension
in intuition, without reproduction in the imagination, then in
some sense the first is second. In the beginning was the begun,
the always already there of a temporality that cannot be traced
as one traces a line, cannot be traced. Neither in consciousness
nor in some region in the depths of the soul that might be called
the unconscious, *in illo tempore*.

What about the third fold, this third complication, of Kant's threefold synthesis: recognition in a concept? The transcendental concepts that condition empirical concepts include the concepts of the three analogies, substance, cause and reciprocity. These are respectively analogies of the permanence of time, that is, time itself, and of the temporal modalities succession and coexistence. Inevitably, if temporality and the constructions of the schematism of imagination that is the milieu between intuitive perception and conception are congenitally contaminated by delay and relay, if what Kant calls self-affection is infected by the primary secondariness at which he himself hints, then the concepts of substance and cause and reciprocity which are for Kant the bounds of sense will only be theoretical and fictive 'effects' of an aboriginal dream-time where representation is older than presentation and presence is perpetually postponed: an uncanny time whose logic, as Freud says of dreams, tolerates contraries and contradiction, 'the original temporality of writing, its "primary" complication: an originary spacing, deferring, and erasure of the simple origin, and polemics on the very threshold of what we persist in calling perception' [*ED* 334 (226)], on the very threshold of conception, on the very threshold of sense.

Post-script: Glassification

atri janua Ditis

Vergil

If the time of writing is the time of imagination, imagination can no longer be simply synthesis, *Einbildungskraft*. It will be construction and deconstruction. And its power of representation, its *Vorstellungsvermögen*, will call for a sense of *vor* that is not the 'before' of presence and presentation. The time of writing is a time that is out of joint, a time in which 'the *simple* structure of maintenance and manuscription, like every intuition of an origin, is a myth' [*ED* 334 (226)]. It is not the time of the phenomenon and phenomenology, the time of a fenced-in field of sense. And its not being this is not just overabundance of meaning, expansive plurisemia, but what makes this possible and impossible: the general economy of the text referred to in Chapter 1, expenditure without consumption or return. What comes to pass in this time of epigraphical inscription is the generation of meaning which is always already divided and is therefore an *a priori* de-generation. Meaning begins endingly, de-limited: 'la dissémination *affirme* la génération toujours déjà divisée du sens. Elle – le laisse d'avance tomber' [*Diss* 300 (268)]. Meaning is allowed to fall – towards its tomb. Dissemination is a generality operator that is the death of generation. It tolls the knell (*glas*) of classification. It is the de-generation of genre, the de-formation of form.

Derrida's strategies raise again Plato's question whether there are forms of filth. This question is reopened in the recto and rectal column of *Glas* and in 'Economimesis'. The latter essay examines the theory of disgust proposed by Kant's third *Critique*. Kant argues there that there is something more disgusting than the gustatorily disgusting, than that which is offensive to taste and therefore belongs to the same system of orality as taste. According to Kant, this something other is what is offensive to

119

the sense of smell. Derrida suggests that Kant is hinting here at what subverts any system of negative opposition, what falls within the range neither of a particular sense nor a concept (in this, incidentally, it is like the Kantian schema). For it all names are lacking. To ask what it is would be to suppose that we can express what it is, but that would be to forget that it does not belong to the system of the oral. It is not containable within any sentence frame. It is *parergonal*. It has no logical form. Rather is it the amorphous and aoristic that deforms form in general.

Hence Derrida's interest in the 'materialism of the idea', as Hyppolite describes one of Mallarmé's themes, though 'theme' is a word that Derrida would recommend we use with prudence of Mallarmé – and of the anagrams of Saussure, his so-called theme words. For the word 'theme' conjures up the picture of a meaning recuperable by a classical hermeneutics which fails to think through to the consequences of the fact that context permeates the text, and that goes for the 'present' context of interpretation 'here and now' (*en ce moment même*). Hence there is a continuous interference effect. Even when it seems that I identify myself by giving my name or identify something as mine, my very own, by apposing my signature, even if I endorse that signature, and endorse the endorsement. Someone else, or I myself may have my signature rewritten as a common name, as Genet does when he begins to sign himself Genêt (where the circumflex accent marks the disappearance of an *s*, the disseminating letter par excellence, according to Mallarmé), as Derrida does for his signature in *Glas*, 'Ellipse' and elsewhere, and as Ponge does when, as Derrida says in *Signéponge*:

> To employ Russellian terminology, we could say that he diabolized his signature, and all the language and the speech it contaminates, because he disguises every proper name as a description and every description as a proper name, showing, by way of this ruse, that such a possibility, always an open one, was constitutive of writing, to the extent that literature works it over on all sides. You never know whether he names or describes, nor whether the thing he describes-names is the thing or the name, the common or proper name. [*S* 118]

What Ponge shows is not just that 'there is a fluctuation in grammar between criteria and symptoms', as illustrated by the

fact that under certain circumstances we are willing to deny that
it is raining even though it feels and looks as though it is.[1] Nor
is the point of what he does that, whether we consider a particular description (for example, 'the man who led the Israelites
through the wilderness') to give the or part of the meaning of the
proper name Moses, or whether we consider this to determine its
reference, someone else may rely on another description (for
example, 'the man who was taken out of the Nile by Pharoah's
daughter') to perform either of these functions.[2] Nor again is the
point that, as Searle and maybe Wittgenstein maintain, either or
both of these functions can be performed by varied clusters from
an open family of such descriptions. The point is that 'there is
always already an internal difference, an element of articulation
or syntax at work in every unit, every identity, even "atomic"'
[*S(C)* 159] which allows an undecidability as to whether someone is talking about a material thing like a porous sponge or an
open-textured and unsaturable name like Ponge, and as to
whether someone is mentioning or using his name or mentioning
or using its. The same kind of undecidability obtains over
whether a word on the page of Mallarmé's *Coup de dés* is an 'ideal'
object with sense or only a 'material' object with only shape and
place.

If it be protested that the poetry and poetic prose of Ponge and
Mallarmé should not be taken as a guide to how words are used
in scientific or philosophic prose, we must remind ourselves that
Derrida is asking whether we understand this distinction and
through his own theory and practice suggesting that we don't. It
is significant that of *Glas* he says that it is neither a philosophical
nor a poetic text, that it attempts to produce another kind of text
of which one can say that it is of another genre or that it is
without genre [*OA* 186]. 'La Loi du genre' argues (yes, argues)
in such a way as to make it clear that Derrida is not just
producing a borderline case, or saying that Ponge and Mallarmé
are producing borderline cases which show how difficult it can
sometimes be to ascribe a text to a class. The difficulty in
question is one that holds not just with borderline cases, but with
the notion of a borderline and the notion of a case, whether
borderline or normal. Our very notion of the self-identity of a
case is called into question. It turns out to be a notion that
undoes itself. For it assumes that for the class formed by class,
form, type, mode, genre, there is a mark that distinguishes

members of that class, whether, for example, a text is a piece of philosophy, a poem, a play or a novel. It tells us to which class it belongs. It may tell us this explicitly, as does Mallarmé's *Coup de dés* in saying after its title: *Poëme*. But it may also tell us its genre through its being in rhyme, through indicating which words come at the beginning and end of a line, or through a definite or indefinite number of such features. But this indicating, although it is an indicating of what, joking apart, makes the text a poem, is not itself poetic. It is not a member of the class poetry even if it is an indicating of what makes a poem a member of that class. Nor is it a simple part of the poem, nor a simple property, if we follow Frege in distinguishing a property (*Eigenschaft*) as a concept under which things fall (e.g. the having of a determinate line-length of which a poem is a case) from a mark (*Merkmal*) as a feature constitutive of a concept (as having a determinate line-length may be held to be constitutive of the concept of poem).[3] It is not a simple property because in telling us that a certain string of words falls under the concept of poetry it at the very same time puts itself outside that concept's scope. While being a property of the poem, determinate line-length deappropriates itself from the poem in so distinguishing itself. Since it is of the essence of a class, for example, poetry, that it indicates what distinguishes it as such, the poem itself will have a part which is apart from itself, a part which is insideoutside. This means that the poem itself, by virtue of that part, will be insideoutside. Inside the genre of poetry and outside it, so not inside one genre and inside another in parallel. The very line which divides a text from its context is divided. Delimitation is de-limited, demarcation de-marcated. The line is crossed [*LG* 184–6 (210-13)].

In view of this argument – though its formality calls for supplementation at least by a reading of the readings of Blanchot that follow it – we can understand why after listening to Derrida's contribution to the Cerisy colloquium on Ponge one participant confessed that he had difficulty determining the status of what he had just heard. Questions of status, Derrida notes, assume a standpoint, a position, a stance (*stanza*: a place where one stays). If his work has a status it is that of a working over of this assumption of what Heidegger refers to in one of his titles as dwelling, *Wohnen*, and thinking, *Denken*, and *Bauen*, construction. It is an investigation of the familiarity of family resemblance, a

reconnaissance, re-con-naissance, of the threshold between semantic home and abroad, a queerying of *Heimlichkeit*, the ownmost (*eigenst*), authenticity, propriety, property, enclosure and
the close. One of the findings of this inquiry is that, for reasons
outlined in 'La Loi du genre', the essence of the close is no closer
than the essence of the red [*Pas* 129]. Propinquity, propriety
and property are effects enshrined in semiological institutes and
legal codes. Even the allegedly inauthentic and false etymologies
that are disseminated on Derrida's pages (it is not especially for
'true' ones that he looks up von Wartburg and Littré) demonstrate how the apparently arbitrary is motivated by 'a desire of
the proper that sets the text in motion once again' so that letters
and words may discover what they will have meant and what we
shall have been obliged to say. There would indeed be no text
but for this desire [*S(C)* 146]. It is this that incites it into life, a
life not of dialectical double negation like the neighing of Za-
rathustra's ass, but a life of double affirmation: amen amen, *oui
oui*, hear hear. Here there. Not here here or there there, *da da*,
but *fort da*. For this life is also an afterlife and a survival, a living
on, on death, a death/life and a life/death. Because the bar is
always already crossed [*S* 114–15]. The operation of the singular
indefinite dyad that engenders gender, genus, genre and generality, the very life of language, of philosophy and the poem, is
uneventful, an *Enteignis*, because it is at one and the same time
[*hama*; *M* 61ff. (53ff.)] their de-generation and death [*Diss* 245
(216)]. Because the very limit is de-limited, the line de-lineated.
Apeiron is *apeiron* of *peras*, where the 'of' is both objective and
subjective: a Janus genitive. The *Merkmal* is a *Denkmal* in memory of the mourning whose death we mourn. The wink of the eye
that sees the first light of sense sees the coming of the 'night of
the secret' (that there is no secret), the dark blank where we
cannot see to see.

Notes and References

CHAPTER 1: DIALECTICAL SEMIOLOGY

1. See John Llewelyn, 'Heidegger's Kant and the Middle Voice', in David Wood and Robert Bernasconi (eds) *Time and Metaphysics* (University of Warwick: Parousia Press, 1982).
2. G. W. F. Hegel, *Encyclopædia*, *Philosophy of Mind*, section 455 (Oxford: Clarendon, 1971) p. 207.
3. Ibid., section 456, *Zusatz*, p. 209.
4. Ibid., section 458, p. 213.
5. Hegel, *Science of Logic* (London: Allen and Unwin, 1969) p. 213.
6. Hegel, *Introduction to Æsthetics*, trans. T. M. Knox, with an interpretative essay by Charles Karelis (Oxford: Clarendon, 1979) p. 88.
7. Ibid.
8. Jean Hyppolite, 'Structure du langage philosophique d'après la Préface de la *Phénoménologie de l'esprit* de Hegel' in Richard Macksey and Eugenio Donato (eds) *The Structuralist Controversy* (Baltimore and London: Johns Hopkins University Press, 1970) p. 343.
9. Hegel, *Phenomenology of Spirit* (Oxford: Clarendon, 1977) p. 142.
10. Hegel, *Encyclopædia*, *Logic*, section 119 (Oxford: Clarendon, 1975) p. 174.
11. Ibid., section 121 (pp. 175–6).
12. Alexandre Koyré, *Etudes d'histoire de la pensée philosophique* (Paris: Gallimard, 1971) p. 168.
13. Jean Hyppolite, *Figures de la pensée philosophique* (Paris: Presses Universitaires de France, 1971) vol. 1, pp. 351–2.
14. As lost as the notes from which Hyppolite spoke about absolute knowing at his seminar on Hegel at the Collège de France. When the proceedings of this seminar were published after his death the volume contained six papers, including Derrida's 'Le Puits et la pyramide', but nothing by the convener himself. See the *Avertissement* of Jacques d'Hondt (ed.) *Hegel et la pensée moderne* (Paris: Presses Universitaires de France, 1970).
15. See Gaston Bachelard, *Essai sur la connaissance approchée* (Paris: Vrin, 1928) p. 270, and *La Formation de l'esprit scientifique* (Paris: Vrin, 1938) p. 239; Thomas S. Kuhn, *The Structure of Scientific Revolutions* (Chicago: University of Chicago, 1962) Chapter 10.

CHAPTER 2: TRANSCENDENTAL PHENOMENOLOGICAL SEMIOLOGY

1. Edmund Husserl, *The Phenomenology of Internal Time Consciousness* (The Hague: Nijhoff, 1964) section 19, p. 69.
2. Ibid., p. 70.
3. Ibid., section 6, p. 39.
4. Ibid., section 13, p. 56.
5. Husserl, *Cartesian Meditations* (The Hague: Nijhoff, 1960) p. 145.
6. Locke, *Essay Concerning Human Understanding*, II, 17, 7. Husserl, *Ideas* (London: Allen and Unwin, 1931) section 143.
7. Husserl, *Ideas*, section 124.
8. Husserl, *Logical Investigations* (London: Routledge and Kegan Paul, 1970) Investigation I, section 5.
9. *Ideas*, section 70.
10. Ibid., section 23.
11. Ibid., section 24.
12. Husserl, *Logical Investigations*, Investigation I, section 8.
13. Husserl, *Ideas*, section 52.
14. Locke, *Essay*, II, 23, 7.
15. The English translation omits the first 'not' in the sentence 'Is being a sign of itself (*index sui*) not the same as not being a sign?'
16. Husserl, *Ideas*, section 43.
17. Husserl, *The Crisis of European Sciences and Transcendental Phenomenology* (Evanston: Northwestern University Press, 1970) p. 360.
18. Husserl, *Logical Investigations*, Investigation I, section 26.
19. Hegel, *Phenomenology of Spirit* (Oxford, Clarendon Press, 1977) p. 62.
20. Husserl, *Logical Investigations*, Investigation I, section 14.
21. J. N. Mohanty, 'On Husserl's Theory of Meaning', *The Southwestern Journal of Philosophy*, V (1974) pp. 229–44.
22. Husserl, *Logical Investigations*, Investigation I, section 15.
23. Husserl, *Ideas*, section 143.
24. Ibid., section 149.
25. Husserl, *Crisis*, p. 363.
26. Husserl, *Logical Investigations*, Investigation I, section 28.
27. Husserl, *Crisis*, p. 362.
28. Husserl, *Logical Investigations*, Investigation VI, chapter 8.
29. Ludwig Wittgenstein, *Tractatus Logico-Philosophicus* (London: Routledge and Kegan Paul, 1961) 5.4541.

CHAPTER 3: FUNDAMENTAL ONTOLOGICAL SEMIOLOGY

1. Martin Heidegger, *The Basic Problems of Phenomenology* (Bloomington: Indiana University Press, 1982) p. 23.
2. Gottlob Frege, *Philosophical Writings* (Oxford: Blackwell, 1952) pp. 45–6.

3. Martin Heidegger, 'Der Spruch des Anaximander', *Holzwege* (Frankfurt-am-Main: Klostermann, 1957) pp. 336–7.
4. Edmund Husserl, *The Phenomenology of Internal Time Consciousness* (The Hague: Nijhoff, 1964) section 36 and part 2, appendix I.

CHAPTER 4: STRUCTURALIST SEMIOLOGY

1. Martin Heidegger, *Holzwege* (Frankfurt-am-Main: Klostermann, 1972) pp. 337–8; cited at *M* 29 (27), *SP* 160.
2. Ferdinand de Saussure, *Course in General Linguistics* (London: Fontana-Collins, 1974) p. 18.
3. Claude Lévi-Strauss, *The Savage Mind* (*La Pensée sauvage*) (London: Weidenfeld and Nicolson, 1966) p. 247. See John Llewelyn, *Beyond Metaphysics? The Hermeneutic Circle in Contemporary Continental Philosophy* (New York: Humanities Press; London: Macmillan, 1985) Chapter 8, section 2.
4. Maine de Biran, *De l'Apperception immédiate* (Paris: Vrin, 1963) pp. 197–8. Cp. *CP* 214: 'By means of this banal gadget [a two-way radio] I should be able to listen to myself talking. And, if you are with me, what I say reaches its destination *a priori*, with all its studied effects. Or again, what comes to the same thing, I find the best way of finding myself *a priori*, in the act of awaiting and reaching myself, wherever it arrives, always here and there at the same time, *fort und da*. Now it always arrives at its destination.'
5. I follow Gayatri Chakravorty Spivak in translating Derrida's *archi-écriture* (and *archi-trace*) by 'arche-writing' (and 'arche-trace'). Although *archi* carries the idea of prince as well as principle whereas *arche* leans more toward principle or origin, and although it is the notion of origin which is to the fore at *G* 90 (61), both prefixes have a common root in *archo*. Of course, Derrida's *archi* is being used under erasure. The original sense is crossed out. The arche-writing or arche-trace is the non-original origin of alleged transcendental origins.

CHAPTER 5: RHETOROLOGICAL SEMIOLOGY

1. L. Wittgenstein, *The Blue and the Brown Books* (Oxford: Blackwell, 1958) pp. 109, 117; cp. *Philosophical Investigations* (Oxford: Blackwell, 1967) 38.
2. J. L. Austin, *How to do things with Words* (Oxford: Clarendon, 1962).
3. John R. Searle, *Speech Acts* (Cambridge: Cambridge University Press, 1969).
4. John R. Searle, 'Reiterating the Differences: A Reply to Derrida', *Glyph*, **1** (1977) pp. 198–208.
5. Austin, *How to do things with Words*, p. 22.
6. Wittgenstein, *Tractatus Logico-Philosophicus* (London: Routledge and Kegan Paul, 1961) 3.23; cp. *Philosophical Investigations*, 9, 27–30, 257.
7. Gilles Deleuze and Félix Guattari, *Rhizomes* (Paris: Minuit, 1976).
8. John R. Searle, 'The Logical Status of Fictional Discourse', *New Literary History*, **5** (1975) p. 319.

9. Translated from Nietzsche, *Le Livre du philosophe* (Paris: Aubier Flammarion, 1969) pp. 181–2, cited at *M* 258 (217).
10. This distinction between concept and conceit was suggested to me by Fergus Kerr.
11. Dugald Stewart, *Philosophical Essays* (Edinburgh: Creech and Constable, 1810) p. 217, cited by J. S. Mill, *System of Logic* (London: Longmans, Green and Co., 1904) p. 442.
12. Pierre Fontanier, *Les Figures du discours* (Paris: Flammarion, 1968) pp. 213–14, cited at *M* 305 (255).
13. Plato, *Sophist* 241d–242a in F. M. Cornford, *Plato's Theory of Knowledge* (London: Routledge and Kegan Paul, 1935) pp. 214–15.

CHAPTER 6: ANASEMIOLOGY

1. See 'La Double séance' in *La Dissémination*.
2. G. W. F. Hegel, *Science of Logic* (London: Allen and Unwin, 1969); p. 107.
3. Hegel, *Encyclopædia, Logic*, section 82, *Zusatz* (Oxford: Clarendon, 1975) p. 121.
4. Ibid., section 96, *Zusatz*, p. 142.
5. Alexandre Koyré, *Etudes d'histoire de la pensée philosophique* (Paris: Gallimard, 1971) p. 212.
6. *Nietzsche aujourd'hui* (Paris: Union Générale d'Editions, 1973) vol. 1, p. 292.
7. F. Nietzsche, *Beyond Good and Evil*, 2 (London: Penguin Books, 1973) p. 16.
8. Gilles Deleuze, *Nietzsche et la philosophie*, (Paris: Presses Universitaires de France, 1970) p. 197.
9. Emile Benveniste, *Problèmes de linguistique générale* (Paris: Gallimard, 1966) vol. 1, p. 172.
10. Jan Gonda, 'Reflections on the Indo-European Medium', *Lingua*, IX (1960) p. 49.
11. Ibid., p. 180.
12. Oswald Szemerényi, *Einführung in die vergleichende Sprachwissenschaft* (Darmstadt: Wissenschaftliche Buchgesellschaft, 1970) p. 232.
13. Sigmund Freud, *Standard Edition of the Complete Psychological Works* (London: Hogarth Press and the Institute of Psycho-analysis, vol. XVII, 1955) pp. 218ff.
14. Ibid., vol. XI, pp. 154ff.
15. Alexander Bain, *Logic* (London: Longmans, Green and Co., 1870) vol. 1, p. 54.
16. Hegel, *Encyclopædia, Logic*, section 96, *Zusatz*, p. 142.
17. David Hume, *An Inquiry Concerning the Principles of Morals*, Appendix III.

CHAPTER 7: THE DIVIDED LINE

1. See Jaakko and Merrill B. Hintikka, 'The Development of Wittgenstein's Philosophy: The Hidden Unity', *Acts of the 7th Wittgenstein Symposium* (Vienna: Hölder-Pichler-Tempsky, 1983) pp. 425ff.

2.   L. Wittgenstein, *Philosophical Investigations* (Oxford: Blackwell, 1967) 289, 290.
3.   Emmanuel Levinas, *Autrement qu'être ou au-delà de l'essence* (The Hague: Nijhoff, 1978) p. 213 [*Otherwise Than Being or Beyond Essence* (The Hague: Nijhoff, 1981) p. 168].
4.   Wittgenstein, *Philosophical Investigations*, 111.
5.   Gottlob Frege, *Philosophical Writings* (Oxford: Blackwell, 1952) pp. 160–1.
6.   Ibid., p. 67.
7.   Wittgenstein, *Philosophical Investigations*, p. 230.
8.   Ibid., 497.
9.   Ibid., 437.
10. Jean Starobinski, *Les Mots sous les mots* (Paris: Gallimard, 1971) p. 154.
11. Wittgenstein, *Philosophical Investigations*, 208.
12. Ibid., 190, 197, 198.
13. Ibid., 560.
14. Derrida, 'Envoi', Actes du XVIIIe Congrès des Sociétés de Philosophie de Langue Française, Strasbourg, 1980 (Paris: Vrin), p. 6 ['Sending: On Representation', *Social Research*, **49** (1982) p. 297].
15. Derrida, 'My Chances/*Mes Chances*: A Rendezvous with Some Epicurean Stereophanies', Joseph H. Smith and William Kerrigan (eds), *Taking Chances: Derrida, Psychoanalysis and Literature* (Baltimore: Johns Hopkins University Press, 1984) p. 21.
16. Derrida, 'Envoi', pp. 29–30 [pp. 325–6].
17. Wittgenstein, *Philosophical Investigations*, 84.
18. Ibid., 88.
19. Ibid., 219.
20. Nelson Goodman, *Fact, Fiction and Forecast* (Indianapolis: Bobbs-Merrill, 1965) pp. 74–5; cp. pp. 79–81, 93–100.
21. Ibid., pp. 96–7.
22. Saul A. Kripke, *Wittgenstein on Rules and Private Language* (Oxford: Blackwell, 1982) p. 20.
23. W. V. Quine, *Ontological Relativity and Other Essays* (New York: Columbia University Press, 1969) p. 48.
24. Ibid., pp. 50–1.
25. G. W. F. Hegel, *Early Theological Writings* (Philadelphia: University of Pennsylvania Press, 1971) pp. 189ff.
26. Maurice Blanchot, *L'Espace littéraire* (Paris: Gallimard, 1955) p. 34.
27. Stéphane Mallarmé, *Oeuvres complètes* (Paris: Gallimard, 1945) p. 387.
28. Gilles Deleuze, *Nietzsche et la philosophie* (Paris: Presses Universitaires de France, 1970) pp. 38–9.
29. A. E. Taylor, *A Commentary on Plato's Timæus* (Oxford: Clarendon Press, 1928) p. 300.
30. A. E. Taylor, *Plato* (London: Methuen, 1949) p. 455.
31. Richard Kearney, *Dialogues with Contemporary Continental Thinkers* (Manchester: Manchester University Press, 1984) p. 119 . Cp. p. 126: 'Deconstruction gives pleasure in that it gives desire. To deconstruct a text is to disclose how it functions as desire, as a search for presence and fulfilment which is interminably deferred. One cannot read without opening oneself to the desire of language, to the search for that which remains absent and other than oneself. Without a certain love of the text, no reading would be

possible. In every reading there is a *corps-à-corps* between reader and text, an incorporation of the reader's desire into the desire of the text. Here is pleasure, the very opposite of that arid intellectualism of which deconstruction has so often been accused.'

32. Richard Rorty, 'Philosophy as a Kind of Writing: An Essay on Derrida', *New Literary History*, **10** (1978) pp. 146–7, cited at Jonathan Culler, *On Deconstruction: Theory and Criticism after Structuralism* (Ithaca: Cornell University Press, 1982; London: Routledge and Kegan Paul, 1983) p. 144.
33. Jean Hyppolite, 'Le *Coup de dés* de Stéphane Mallarmé et le message', *Etudes philosophiques*, **13** (1958) p. 466.
34. Gayatri Chakravorty Spivak, '*Glas*-Piece: a Compte Rendu', *Diacritics*, **7** (1977) p. 26.
35. Immanuel Kant, *Critique of Pure Reason*, A 97.

POST-SCRIPT: GLASSIFICATION

1. Wittgenstein, *Philosophical Investigations* (Oxford: Blackwell, 1967) 354.
2. Ibid., 87.
3. Gottlob Frege, *Philosophical Writings* (Oxford: Blackwell, 1952) pp. 51, 145.

Bibliography

1. Derrida's publications referred to in the text

BSF   'La Différance', *Bulletin de la Société Française de Philosophie*, **62** (1968) 73–101, Discussion 101–20 [Discussion in David Wood and Robert Bernasconi (eds) *Derrida and Differance* (University of Warwick: Parousia Press, 1985)].

CP   *La Carte postale* (Paris: Aubier-Flammarion, 1980).

Diss   *La Dissémination* (Paris: Seuil, 1972). [*Dissemination*, trans. Barbara Johnson (Chicago: University of Chicago Press, 1981; London: Athlone Press, 1981)].

ECM   'En ce moment même dans cet ouvrage me voici', in François Laruelle (ed.) *Textes pour Emmanuel Levinas* (Paris: Jean-Michel Place, 1980) pp. 21–60.

ED   *L'Ecriture et la différence* (Paris: Seuil, 1967). [*Writing and Difference*, trans. Alan Bass (Chicago: University of Chicago Press, 1978; London: Routledge and Kegan Paul, 1978)].

Fors   'Fors: les mots anglés de Nicolas Abraham et Maria Torok', Introduction to Nicolas Abraham and Maria Torok, *Cryptonymie: le Verbier de l'homme aux loups* (Paris: Aubier-Flammarion, 1976) pp. 7–73. [Trans. Barbara Johnson, *The Georgia Review*, **31** (1977) 64–116].

G   *De la grammatologie* (Paris: Minuit, 1967). [*Of Grammatology*, trans. Gayatri Chakravorty Spivak (Baltimore and London: The Johns Hopkins University Press, 1974, 1976)].

Glas   *Glas* (Paris: Galilée, 1974) [also *Glas* (Paris: Denoël/Gonthier, 1981)].

Ja   'Ja, ou le faux-bond', *Digraphe*, **11** (1977) 83–121. See 'Entre crochets' below.

LG   'La Loi du genre', *Glyph*, **7** (1980) 176–201 ['The Law of Genre', trans. Avital Ronell, ibid., 202–29].

LI   'Limited Inc a b c . . .', *Glyph*, **2**, Supplement (Baltimore and London: Johns Hopkins University Press, 1977). [Trans. Samuel Weber, *Glyph*, **2** (1977) 162–254].

M   *Marges de la philosophie* (Paris: Minuit, 1972). [*Margins of Philosophy*, trans. Alan Bass (Chicago: University of Chicago Press, 1982; Brighton: Harvester Press, 1982)].

O   Introduction to Edmund Husserl, *L'Origine de la géométrie* (Paris: Presses Universitaires de France, 1962. [Introduction to Edmund Husserl, *The Origin of Geometry*, trans. John P. Leavey (Stony Brook: Nicolas Hays, 1978; Brighton: Harvester Press, 1978)].

OA   *L'Oreille de l'autre* (Montreal: VLB Editeur, 1982) [pp. 134, 49–56: 'All

Ears: Nietzsche's Otobiography', trans. Avital Ronell, *Yale French Studies*, **63** (1982) 245–50].

Pas   'Pas', *Gramma*, **3/4** (1976) 111–215.

Pos   *Positions* (Paris: Minuit, 1972). [*Positions*, trans. Alan Bass (Chicago: University of Chicago Press, 1981; London: Athlone Press, 1981)].

S   *Signéponge/Signsponge*, trans. Richard Rand (New York: Columbia University Press, 1984).

S(C)   'Signéponge', in *Ponge: Inventeur et classique*, Colloque de Cerisy (Paris: Union générale d'éditions, 1977) pp. 115–51. See 'Signéponge' below.

Sec   'signature événement contexte', *M*, pp. 365–93 ['Signature Event Context', trans. Samuel Weber and Jeffrey Mehlman, *Glyph*, **1** (1977) 172–97].

SP   *Speech and Phenomena*, trans. David B. Allison (Evanston: Northwestern University Press, 1973).

Spurs   *Spurs: Nietzsche's Styles/Eperons: Les Styles de Nietzsche*, trans. Barbara Harlow (Chicago: University of Chicago Press, 1979). [Also *Eperons: Les Styles de Nietzsche* (Paris: Flammarion, 1978)].

VEP   *La Vérité en peinture* (Paris: Flammarion, 1978). [*Truth in Painting*, trans. Geoff Bennington and Ian McLeod (Chicago: University of Chicago Press, 1985)].

VP   *La Voix et le phénomène* (Paris: Presses Universitaires de France, 1967) [*SP*].

2. Other publications by Derrida

'L'Age de Hegel', in GREPH, *Qui a peur de la philosophie?* (Paris: Flammarion, 1977) pp. 73–107.

L'Archéologie du frivole: Lire Condillac (Paris: Denoël/Gonthier, 1976). [*The Archæology of the Frivolous: Reading Condillac*, trans. John P. Leavey (Pittsburgh: Duquesne University Press, 1980)].

'Avoir l'oreille de la philosophie', in Lucette Finas et al., *Ecarts: Quatre essais à propos de Jacques Derrida* (Paris: Fayard, 1973), pp. 303–12.

'Choreographies', interview with Christie V. McDonald, *Diacritics*, **12** (1982) 66–76.

'Deconstruction and the other', interview with Richard Kearney, in Richard Kearney, *Dialogues with Contemporary Continental Thinkers* (Manchester: Manchester University Press, 1984) pp. 105–126.

'Deux mots pour Joyce' (Paris: L'Herne, forthcoming). ['Two words for Joyce', trans. Geoff Bennington, in Derek Attridge and Daniel Ferrer (eds), *Post-structuralist Joyce: essays from the French* (Cambridge: Cambridge University Press, 1984) pp. 145–59].

'Devant la loi', in A. Phillips Griffiths (ed.) *Philosophy and Literature* (Cambridge: Cambridge University Press, 1984) pp. 173–88.

'Economimesis', in Sylviane Agacinski et al., *Mimesis des articulations* (Paris: Aubier-Flammarion, 1975) pp. 57–93.

'Entre crochets', *Digraphe*, **8** (1976) 97–114 [continued in *Ja*, see above].

'Envoi', Actes du XVIIIe Congrès des Sociétés de Philosophie de Langue Française, Strasbourg, 1980 (Paris: Vrin) pp. 6–30. ['Sending: On Representation', trans. Peter and Mary Ann Caws, *Social Research*, **49** (1982) 294–326].

'Geschlecht: différence sexuelle, différence ontologique', in Michel Haar (ed.) *Heidegger* (Paris: L'Herne, 1983) pp. 419–30. ['Geschlecht: sexual difference, ontological difference,' *Research in Phenomenology*, **13** (1983) 65–83].

'Geschlecht (II): La main de l'homme selon Heidegger', in John Sallis (ed.) Proceedings of the 1985 Loyola University of Chicago conference on 'Deconstruction and Philosophy', forthcoming.

An interview with Jacques Derrida (James Kearns and Ken Newton), *The Literary Review*, **14** (1980) 21–2.

Letter to a Japanese Friend, in David Wood and Robert Bernasconi (eds) *Derrida and Differance* (University of Warwick: Parousia Press, 1985).

'Living On: Border Lines', trans. James Hulbert, in Harold Bloom et al., *Deconstruction and Criticism* (New York: Seabury, 1979) pp. 75–176.

'Mallarmé', in *Tableau de la littérature française: De Madame de Staël à Rimbaud* (Paris: Gallimard, 1974) pp. 368–79.

'Mochlos ou le conflit des facultés', *Philosophie*, **2** (1984) 21–53. ['The Conflict of Faculties', in Michael Riffatere (ed.) *Languages of Knowledge and Inquiry* (New York: Columbia University Press, announced)].

'Moi-la psychanalyse', *Confrontation*, **8** (1982) 5–15. ['Me-Psychoanalysis: An Introduction to the Translation of "The Shell and the Kernel" by Nicolas Abraham', trans. Richard Klein, *Diacritics*, **9** (1979) 4–12.]

'Les Morts des Roland Barthes', *Poétique*, **47** (1981) 269–92.

'My Chances/*Mes Chances*: A Rendezvous with Some Epicurean Stereophanies', trans. Irene Harvey and Avital Ronell, in Joseph H. Smith and William Kerrigan (eds) *Taking Chances: Derrida, Psychoanalysis, and Literature* (Baltimore and London: Johns Hopkins University Press, 1984) pp. 1–32.

'Ocelle comme pas un', Preface to Jos Joliet, *L'Enfant au chien-assis* (Paris: Galilée, 1980).

'Où commence et comment finit un corps enseignant', in Dominique Grisoni (ed.) *Politiques de la philosophie* (Paris: Grasset, 1976) pp. 55–97.

'La Phénoménologie et la clôture de la métaphysique', *Epoches* (1966).

'Philosophie: Derrida l'insoumis', *Le Nouvel Observateur*, 9 September 1983, pp. 84–9 [Interview with *Le Nouvel Observateur*, in David Wood and Robert Bernasconi (eds) *Derrida and Differance* (University of Warwick: Parousia Press, 1985)].

'Philosophie des Etats Généraux', in *Etats Généraux de la philosophie (16 et 17 juin 1979)* (Paris: Flammarion, 1979) pp. 27–44 and *passim*.

'La Philosophie et ses classes', in GREPH, *Qui a peur de la philosophie?* (Paris: Flammarion, 1977) pp. 445–450.

'The Principle of Reason: The University in the Eyes of its Pupils', *Diacritics*, **13** (1983) 3–20.

'Réponse à la Nouvelle Critique', in GREPH, *Qui a peur de la philosophie?* (Paris: Flammarion, 1977) pp. 451–8.

'Response to Questions on the Avant-Garde', *Digraphe*, **6** (1975) 152–3.

'Le Retrait de la métaphore', *Poésie*, **6** (1979) 103–26 ['The Retreat of Metaphor', *Enclitic*, **2** (1978) 5–34].

'Scribble', (pouvoir/écrire)' Introduction to William Warburton, *L'Essai sur les hiéroglyphes* (Paris: Flammarion, 1978) ['Scribble (writing-power)', trans. Cary Plotkin, *Yale French Studies*, **59** (1979) 116–47].

'Signéponge', *Digraphe*, **8** (1976) 17–39. Second part of *S(C)*, see above.
'Speculations-On Freud', trans. Ian McLeod, *Oxford Literary Review*, **3** (1978) 78–97.
'D'un texte à l'écart', *Les Temps Modernes*, **25** (1970) 1546–52.
'D'un ton apocalyptique adopté naguère en philosophie', in Philippe Lacoue-Labarthe and Jean-Luc Nancy, *Les Fins de l'homme: à partir du travail de Jacques Derrida* (Paris: Galilée, 1981) pp. 445–86 and elsewhere [also *D'un ton apocalyptique adopté naguère en philosophie* (Paris: Galilée, 1983)].
'The time of a thesis', trans Kathleen McLaughlin, in Alan Montefiore (ed.) *Philosophy in France Today* (Cambridge: Cambridge University Press, 1983) pp. 34–50.
'Titre (à préciser)', *Nuove Corrente*, **28** (1981) 7–32 ['Title (to be specified)', *Sub Stance*, **31** (1978) 5–22].

For further bibliographical information see: John Leavey and David B. Allison, A Derrida Bibliography, *Research in Phenomenology*, **8** (1978) 145–160 [also in *O* 1978, pages 181–93, see above]; Jonathan Culler, *On Deconstruction: Theory and Criticism after Structuralism* (Ithaca: Cornell University Press, 1982; London: Routledge and Kegan Paul, 1983) pp. 281–302.

Index

(prepared by Margo Taylor)

disambiguation, 98
displacement, 13, 15
dissemination, xiii, 10, 11, 70, 94,
117, 119, 120
Donato, E., 9, 10
Dreyfus, H., 73
Dummett, M., 51
dwelling, 122

economy, restricted and general, 11
Ent-fernung, 95
Enteignis, 95
entrenchment, 110, 112
Entschlossenheit, 95
Er-innerung, xii
Ereignis, 34, 84
eschatology, 15, 31
existentialism, 35

family resemblance, 69, 76
Fate, 113
Fichte, J. G., 5
fiction, 67
Fontanier, P., 78
force, 103
forgetting, 111
Foucault, M., 50, 73
Frege, G., xi, xiii, 37, 69, 100, 104,
105, 117, 122
Freud, S., 71, 73, 94–6, 117, 118
Freudian slip, 73
frivolous, 102
fundamental ontology, 86

general economy, 11
Genet, J., 60, 115, 116, 120
glyptography, 3
God, 100, 113
Gödel, K., 88, 115
Gonda, J., 90–3
Goodman, N., 83, 109, 112, 113
grafting (*greffe*), 69
grammatology, 54, 57, 58
graphematics, 57, 59, 64, 65
Guattari, F., 63

Handlung, 101
Hartman, G., 73
hazard, 107

Hegel G. W. F., x–xiii, 1–15, 23, 25,
26, 32, 34–6, 41, 42, 45, 46, 48,
51, 53, 54, 63, 68, 71, 73, 75, 79,
81, 83, 84, 94, 95, 97, 104, 112,
114, 116, 117
Heidegger, M., x, xi, xiii, 9, 10, 13,
16, 32–42, 45, 53–5, 68, 71, 73,
78, 79, 84, 86, 93–5, 101, 111,
112, 115, 116, 122
heimlich, 94, 95
Heimlichkeit, 94, 95, 103, 123
Heraclitus, x, 85, 113, 115
hermeneutics, 120
history, 103, 117
Homer, 2
humanism, 35, 36, 51
Hume, D., 17, 97, 99, 102
Husserl, E., x, xi, 15–31, 37, 41, 42,
45–8, 51, 53–5, 59, 64, 68, 70, 71,
73, 79, 81, 84, 90, 93, 101, 112,
117
hymen, 26, 87, 94, 99, 113, 116
Hyppolite, J., 4, 5, 8–11, 14, 114,
115, 120

Idea in the Kantian sense, 18, 29,
31, 40
identity, 6
illocutionary act, 61
illocutionary force, 67
illusion, transcendental, xii, 48
imagination, 1, 2, 16, 17, 20, 116,
117, 119
indication, 20, 21, 26–8, 62
infinity, 18
inside and outside, xiii, 27, 83, 94,
122
intention, 62, 66, 72, 75
intertextuality, 112
iterability, 27, 62–4, 69, 70, 72, 81

Jentsch, E., 95

Kant, I., xiii, 1, 3, 5, 30, 35, 40, 45,
51, 63, 86, 114, 116–20
Kierkegaard, S., 90
Knight, R. P., 76, 104
Konstruktion, xiii